GREEN MARKETING

Opportunity for Innovation

To Bennadette, all the best Jacquie Ottman 4/7/09

Second Edition

JACQUELYN A. OTTMAN

Foreward by
WILLIAM R. REILLY
Former Administrator, U.S. Environmental Protection Agency

For Stella Kupferberg, with thanks

No finer citizen ever came to a country.
No finer neighbor ever moved onto a block.
No finer friend ever shared a meal.
No finer human being ever shone on a planet.

Contents

Acknowledgments

Like a true green marketing program, this book represents the combined input of many of my personal and professional stakeholders in the realms of industry, government, and nonprofit groups. Several individuals, too many to mention, provided valuable information and case study examples. Others gave generously of their time to review the manuscript or provide other support. To them I extend deepest appreciation: David Balkcom, Gordon Binder, Jill Boekell, C. Anthony di Benedetto, Jocelyne DesPatis, Glenda Goehrs, Caroline Johnson (who also provided invaluable input on the book's organization), Richard Kashmanian, Byron Kennard, Steven Mojo, Leonard Rubin, Robert Stull, Susan Svoboda, Jill Vohr, and Martin Wolf.

Brad Fay and Christopher Rigney of Roper Starch Worldwide were most generous with their research and careful review of the manuscript. Regis Park of Tom's of Maine, Lu Setnicka of Patagonia, and Nancy Hirschberg of Stonyfield Farm guided the development of their company's in-depth case studies.

Last, my deepest appreciation goes to Stacy Bobroff, Ted de Bonis, Rachel Reiss, Peter Resch, Amanda Rhea, Virginia Terry, Aien Thlick, and Jean Wang who did a superb job researching and writing the case studies, among other tasks. I am also indebted to Jen Durci and Debbie Graham who did all the word processing.

Foreword

When I was administrator of the Environmental Protection Agency, during a visit to Cincinnati to inspect one of the Agency's premier laboratories, I stopped by the headquarters of Procter & Gamble. P&G's chief executive, Ed Artzt, proudly displayed for me his company's latest products and recounted the environmental benefits: concentrated detergents that saved energy and transport costs, compostable diapers, recyclable plastic packaging. These products reduced waste, lowered materials use, saved money, and improved the company's image, Artzt said. But P&G wasn't making them because I said to, or because regulations made them do so. Increasingly, consumers the world over demanded them, he said. The market was driving P&G to greener products.

His remark encapsulated for me the new, more environmentally sensitive business climate in which American firms must compete today. It's not enough to refrain from damaging the environment or to be in compliance with environmental laws. The consumer wants to see environmental benefits in the products. New product lines testify to the profound power of the marketplace to drive environmental performance beyond compliance. Smart CEOs and progressive companies get it. They are leaving behind those companies whose goals are limited to staying out of trouble with environmental regulators.

By now it is clear to many corporations that environmental principles are emerging as a critical part of doing business and conducting our lives. Many companies are recycling, conserving energy, and cutting down waste. Consumers are recycling, too, and looking for greener goods when they shop.

One reason I find *Green Marketing: Opportunity for Innovation* so stimulating is that it distills for us in highly readable fashion, drawing on numerous examples, some of the best thinking about creative, effective strategies businesses are adopting to put them and their products on a more environmentally responsible path. These companies are tapping into Americans' abiding concern for environmental quality, a cause that is gaining momentum the world over. More and more, we will see this kind of thinking distinguish the enterprises that will prosper in the dynamic, global marketplace of the 21st century.

William K. Reilly
Chairman, Aqua International Partners
Administrator, U.S. EPA, 1989–1993

Preface

Since the first edition of *Green Marketing* was published in 1993, green shopping has virtually disappeared from newspaper headlines, and "the environment" has been displaced from the top of the public's worry list by such other pressing issues as crime, drugs, the economy, and AIDS. However, such developments do not mean that consumers no longer care about the environmental impact of the products they buy. A peek inside voting booths, shopping carts, and recycling bins will prove that people are acting upon their environmental concerns now more than ever.

Since the late 1980s and early 1990s, anxiety over environmental ills like ozone layer depletion, oil spills, and overflowing landfills has subsided and day-to-day eco-related activities have become the norm. Record numbers of consumers now recycle, seek out eco-labels, and incorporate any number of other environmentally sensitive behaviors into their lives. Businesses now do more than ever to address green, too. They recycle and look for ways to cut down on waste and save energy. Motivated by a growing recognition that environmental and economic goals can work hand in hand, many now-enlightened managers look for ways to green up their products and create win-win alliances with one-time adversaries in government and environmental advocacy groups.

After a misguided attempt at green advertising and claim-making in the 1980s and early 1990s that nearly derailed the modern-day environmental consumerism movement, marketers are finally getting green marketing right. Bolstered by guidelines proffered by the U.S. Federal Trade Commission, marketers now communicate their environmental product initiatives without risk of misleading or confusing their eco-conscious consumers. With the luxury of a raft of green product successes (as well as failures) to learn from and the benefit of time and refined technologies, they introduce products and services that balance consumers' primary needs for quality, convenience, and affordability with environmental soundness. Indeed, environmental performance is now a critical factor in most product developers' design criteria. Conventional marketing is out. Green marketing is in.

Addressing today's sophisticated green consumers requires new strategies and the power to innovate. For readers for whom this book is intended — manufacturers and marketers of consumer products and services and their advertising, public relations, and promotion agency counterparts, as well as entrepreneurs looking to seize opportunities, this edition will serve as an update on the status of the environmental consumerism trend. Using case studies of the most successful green companies, products, programs, and advertising, it will guide your planning and help maximize your opportunities by highlighting the strategies most associated with addressing this trend profitably. Most important, it will underscore the many specific opportunities that innovative green strategies provide for revitalizing your company, renewing your product lines, and recharging the morale of your employees and colleagues.

My personal goal in writing this book is to help skew the market to environmentally preferable products and services and to help people lead more environmentally sustainable and satisfying lives. My hope is that the information and insights shared within can accelerate this global shift and, in the process, reward its primary actors.

Jacquelyn A. Ottman
President, J. Ottman Consulting, Inc., New York City

Greener than Ever

The marketplace is greener now than ever before—and will become even more responsive to products and services promising environmental responsibility well into the 21st century. The reasons are many.

PEOPLE ARE WORRIED

In the 1980s environmental calamities dominated the news. Almost daily, headlines trumpeted oil spills, toxic-waste dumps, and nuclear meltdowns. A hole punctured the ozone layer, a garbage barge searched in vain for a dumpsite, apples were not considered safe to eat. The issues were no longer in someone else's backyard far-away, but in our own.

The environment rose to the top of the public's worry list. Children picketed the United Nations with "Ronald McToxic" in effigy. The 20th-anniversary celebration of Earth Day in 1990 attracted 100 million participants around the world, and *Time* magazine named spaceship Earth, "Planet of the Year."

Government responded. Fueled by voters' fears of discarded eggshells, pantyhose, and other trash creeping up the back step, municipalities banned fast-food cartons from landfills and tried to tax disposable diapers. In Maine, aseptic juice boxes were swept from grocery shelves because they were not broadly recycled. To preserve its markets and safeguard its reputation, industry quickly greened up its products and issued environmental communiqués and ads asserting its commitment to a cleaner Earth.

Consumers felt listened to. They began to recycle their Pepsi cans and aluminum foil, cut down on disposables, and take other environmental steps that gave them a sense of control over their day-to-day lives.

The environment-related hysteria of the late 1980s and early 1990s is now behind us, but consumers' desire to quell their concerns is actually higher now than at the peak of the eco-craze. Their motivation: trepidation for what they see as a very shaky future.

Since the 1980s, the headlines have shifted away from wandering garbage barges and medical waste washing up on the New Jersey shore to genetic breakthroughs and Hollywood murders. However, people still worry about any number of such specific environmental issues as industrial air and water pollution, ozone layer depletion, radiation from nuclear power plants, and destruction of rain forests (see Exhibit 1.1).

We are not alone. Pessimism over the state of the environment reigns in virtually every corner of the world. A 1995 Roper/International Research Associates poll of more than 35,000 adults in 40 countries on five continents—one of the most comprehensive global surveys conducted to date—found that three times as many people worldwide think their country's environmental situation is close to—or is—the worst possible as opposed to the best possible (25 percent versus 8 percent). At 17 percent, North America has its share of adults who believe the environmental situation will be worse—or near the worst possible state—in five years. However, and most likely due to North America's relatively cleaner environment, these figures pale in comparison to the acute pessimism that prevails in the former USSR countries, Latin America, and the Middle East (see Exhibit 1.2).

Exhibit 1.1
"Very Serious" Environmental Concerns

Percent describing as "very serious" problems

Concern	Percent
Industrial water pollution	55%
Destruction of ozone	53%
Destruction of rain forests	53%
Industrial accidents	53%
Hazardous waste	52%
Oil spills	52%
Industrial air pollution	52%
Radiation from nuclear power-plant accidents	52%
Drinking-water contamination	51%
Ocean contamination	50%
Auto air pollution	50%
Endangered species	47%
Pesticides on food	44%
Greenhouse effect	43%
Solid waste	42%
Destruction of wetlands	42%
Acid rain	34%
Biotechnology	34%
Indoor air pollution from household cleaners, tobacco smoke, asbestos, etc.	33%
Indoor air pollution from radon	30%

Source: Roper Starch Worldwide, Green Gauge, 1996. Used with permission

Exhibit 1.2
Global Optimism and Pessimism

Optimists: Percentage who believe their country's environment will be the best or near best possible five years from now.

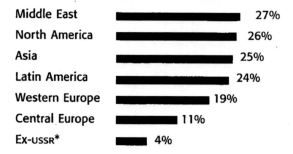

Middle East	27%
North America	26%
Asia	25%
Latin America	24%
Western Europe	19%
Central Europe	11%
Ex-USSR*	4%

Pessimists: Percentage who believe their country's environment will be the worst or near worst possible five years from now.

Ex-USSR*	65%
Latin America	44%
Middle East	42%
Central Europe	35%
Asia	30%
Western Europe	26%
North America	17%

* In this study, Russia and the Ukraine

Source: Roper/International Research Associates Global Study, 1995.
Chart: Green Business Letter, *September, 1995. Tilden Press, Inc. Used with permission*

Count on things to get worse. No corner of the globe escapes the by-products of the one-two punch of rapid global industrialization and burgeoning population growth. Such ills as contaminated water, filthy air, and a decrease in the biological diversity that keeps Earth's ecosystem in balance are more prominent in areas without a history of environmental protection such as Eastern Europe and Asia. Just over the millennial horizon lurks the specter of global climate change and a stratospheric ozone layer that may be too thin to shield the planet from the sun's cancer-causing, crop-depleting UV A and B rays. No wonder that almost two in three people (64 percent) around the world believe "protecting the environment is the most important concern, even at the expense of economic growth," and pro-environment sentiment is mirrored in every region of the world.[1]

Environmentalism Is a Core Societal Value

Environmental consumerism is driven by the largest demographic group in the history of America—the now-maturing Baby Boom population. Representing nearly one-third of the U.S. population, and ranging in age from 30 to 50, the Baby Boomers—Bill Clinton, Bill Gates, and Fred Krupp of the Environmental Defense Fund among them—now dominate society. The deep-rooted values established in their youth shape their lifestyles and decisions.

Recall that the Baby Boomers were the first health- and fitness-conscious generation. They were the recipients of President John F. Kennedy's Presidential Awards for Physical Fitness. That consciousness now merges with their reignited environmental concerns to create a more holistic "wellness" philosophy that emphasizes overall quality of life.

The eldest Boomers led the activist movements of the late 1960s and early 1970s—anti-war, anti–big business, and pro-environment. With Harvard Law School dropout Denis Hayes in charge, it was the Baby Boomers who created the first Earth Day in 1970. The Endangered Species Act of 1973, the Clean Air Act of 1970, and the Clean Water Act of 1972 all sprang from their demonstrated concern.

It is no coincidence that the Baby Boomer–led Clinton Administration has put the environment on its priority list. Although its environmental record is not perfect, such efforts as the U.S. Environmental Protection Agency's Common Sense Initiative, and the Global Climate Change Action Plan, like Al Gore's book, *Earth in the Balance*, demonstrate a desire to balance environmental cleanup with sound economics. Since the Baby Boomers' share of Congress is projected to peak in 2015, we can expect the environment to stay firmly entrenched on the political agenda well into the next millennium.

CITIZENS ARE RESPONDING

There's a sense of betrayal in the air. Citizens acknowledge government's and industry's greener hands, but still feel that all too often politics and profits get in the way of all-out efforts to purify the environment. However, they are not content to stand aside. Individuals know their materialistic consumption contributes to the mess; activist to the core, the Baby Boomer–led citizenry has decided to put their leaders on notice and take things into their own hands.

Nearly half of all U.S. adults now recycle their Coke bottles and morning newspapers. Although not always for altruistic reasons, many Americans pick up after litterbugs, compost yard trimmings, or take their used motor oil to recycling centers. In 1995, more than one-quarter of U.S. voters (27 percent) pulled the lever for candidates based completely or in part on their track records for environmental responsibility, up from 21 percent in 1994. A similar number (26 percent, up from 18 percent in 1993) say they have done volunteer work for the environment.[2]

Peter D. Hart Associates, the Washington, D.C., polling firm, finds that despite a growing impetus for a balanced legislative approach, most voters believe current laws and regulations do not go far enough and are prepared to vote for stiff environmental laws if necessary. Such attitudes predominate—particularly among women, voters age 18 to 34, minorities, and urban dwellers—despite the greater concern they have about such issues as the economy, jobs, taxes, and the cost of living.

GREEN PRODUCT SALES SOAR

America's environmental ethic makes emission-control gasoline, water-saving washing machines and dishwashers, phosphate-free laundry powder, and mercury-free and rechargeable batteries the new gold standards in their respective product categories. As detailed throughout this book, America's love affair with recycling has created markets for recycled building products, packaging, stationery, and even sweaters and sneakers. The solid waste crisis fuels sales of backyard composters, mulchers, and yard-waste bags, while a raised energy consciousness spurs the growth of more efficient appliances, lighting, and heating and cooling systems in homes and offices. Health-conscious consumers fuel markets for organic foods, natural cleaning and personal-care products, air- and water-filtration devices, water-based paints (low-fume) and stains, bottled water, and organic fertilizers and integrated pest management systems that do not rely on man-made chemicals at all. Given current developments, consumers in the early years of the 21st century will be snapping up cars run on electricity or natural gas and home power systems fueled by solar or geothermal energy.

Thanks to new product introductions and more generous allocations of retail space, sales in natural-products outlets of such greener products as environmentally preferable cleaners, "tree-free" paper products, and natural personal-care products are skyrocketing. Gone are the dimly lit general-type stores with cluttered aisles, bulk bins, and limp organic vegetables. In their place are scores of cheery health-food and specialty stores that carry a dizzying array of branded natural foods and green general merchandise.

Exhibit 1.3
Organic Industry Sales Trends

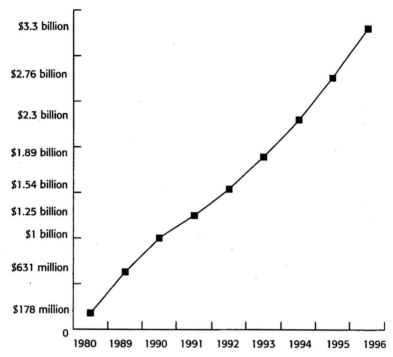

Source: In Business *magazine, November/December 1996, p. 9, and July/August 1995, p. 18*

In 1991, *In Business* magazine, the handbook of eco-entrepreneurs, counted 11 green retailers in the United States. Five years later, at least 400 environmental-product emporiums with such names as Earth General and Ozone Brothers thrive from Boston to Sausalito and dozens of cities in between, and virtual counterparts pop up on the World Wide Web. Gleaming natural-foods supermarkets dominated by the Whole Foods and Fresh Fields chains with estimated sales of $500 million and $200 million each in 1995, compete with Alfalfa's, Wild Oats, and other stores as well as nearly 5,000 mostly small independent operators for an estimated $7.5 billion in yearly sales.[3]

Riding high on this buoyant wave of green shopping, Seventh Generation has branched out from a direct-mail catalog serving the needs of the most ardent green shoppers to a mass marketer of nationally distributed green goods dubbed "Products for a Healthy Planet." Propelled by the wider range of customers who now purchase green products, their sales were $5.1 million in 1996, up 62 percent over 1995. As suggested by surveys of specialty green stores, these customers include the parents of elementary-school children, more older customers, and people with environment-related health problems who are looking for alternative products.[4]

According to Roper Starch Worldwide, "hot" social issues like the environment pass through three distinct phases:

Phase 1: Anxiety is high, activities are relatively low.

Phase 2: People become more informed about the issue and activity overtakes anxiety.

Phase 3: Activities become integrated into people's lifestyles.

Green consumerism is now largely in this second phase. Anxiety is down and behavior is up, albeit confined to the lifestyles of the most environmentally aware. The natural progression for a social issue like environmental concern is to move to Phase 3. For that to happen, mainstream consumers will need greater access to credible, actionable information, technologies, and infrastructures that make it easier for them to behave in an environmentally responsible way. When these developments occur, environmental responsibility could become a way of life for as many as two out of three consumers.[5]

CHILDREN ARE GREEN

No parent or teacher would deny that the environment weighs heavily on the minds of America's naturally idealistic young people. Indeed, the environment is of higher priority to children than to adults. A nationwide research study commissioned by the National

Environmental Education Training Foundation in December 1994 found that youngsters placed the environment third in a list of 10 issues of concern behind AIDS and kidnapping, in contrast to adults, for whom the economy, crime, and drugs hold greater sway. Children in particular fret over long-term issues such as damage to the ozone layer and destruction of the rain forest.

Ninety-nine percent of America's children now have access to environmental classes in school, and 31 states require schools to incorporate environmental concepts into virtually every subject in all grade levels.[6] Education breeds concern and action, particularly among preteens who pitch in on neighborhood cleanups and do their best to skew family grocery-shopping budgets—now upward of $30 billion—toward greener goods. Parents change their shopping habits because their children say certain products are better or worse for the environment than others. The opportunities for greener products will grow as ecologically vigilant children and teens replace the less-green elderly in workplaces, voting booths, and supermarket checkout lines in the years and decades ahead.

TRADING PARTNERS ARE GREEN

In the 1980s, the accidental release of toxic chemicals into the Rhine River, the spread of a nuclear cloud from Chernobyl across Europe, and countless other ecological disasters rocketed awareness of environmental issues into the headlines and onto the political agenda of nations around the world. Such incidents as French nuclear testing in the South Pacific, growing widespread environmental degradation, and the mounting solid-waste issues that continue to plague Germany, Switzerland, the Netherlands, and the United Kingdom keep it there in the 1990s.

The European Directive on Packaging and Packaging Waste passed in late 1994 has already spawned a flurry of stiff recycling and waste-management laws and initiatives with implications around the globe. Germany's experiment with "extended producer responsibility" laws requiring manufacturers to assume control of their products' eventual recycling or responsible disposal has spread far beyond Europe. The potential for such laws in the United States and the economic benefits they provide have made "product take-back" and design for disassembling and recycling a top priority for Xerox, IBM, Hewlett-Packard, and other electronics and appliance manufacturers worldwide.

All over the world manufacturers gear up to become certified with ISO 14001, the first of a series of international voluntary environmental-quality standards that promise to forever change the way business is conducted[7] (see Exhibit 1.4). Eco-labels sponsored by governmental or quasi-governmental agencies decorate products and packages in Germany, Japan, Canada, and 25 other countries.

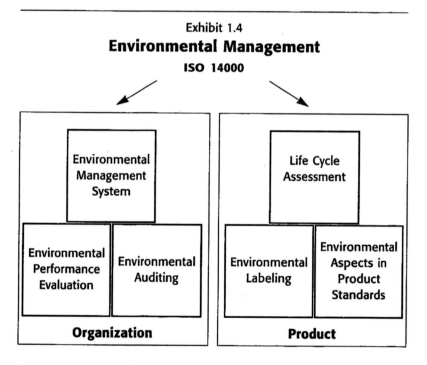

Exhibit 1.4
Environmental Management
ISO 14000

Environmental Management System

Life Cycle Assessment

Environmental Performance Evaluation

Environmental Auditing

Environmental Labeling

Environmental Aspects in Product Standards

Organization

Product

Source: International Organization for Standardization. Chart: Quality Digest, *July 1994. Used with permission*

GREEN MARKETING OPPORTUNITIES

Equipped with a better grasp of ecological issues, enlightened businesspeople voluntarily adopt environmentally responsible business practices. A growing number of CEOs now appreciate the link between environmental responsibility and more efficient—and profitable—business practices. And more and more business communicators know how to use green marketing strategies to take advantage of opportunities to boost their corporate environmental images.

More Profits

Many companies, and especially those in such highly polluting industries as chemicals, oil, and electrical power generation, now have management systems in place to make sure corporate environmental profiles and products exceed consumers' expectations. Today, major U.S. corporations conduct environmental audits and recycle their waste. Countless others upgrade their facilities with energy-efficient technologies. Such steps reduce operating costs and liability while boosting profits.

Producing eco-efficient products creates less waste, uses fewer raw materials, and saves energy, too. Thanks to innovative manufacturing processes suggested by highly motivated and environmentally trained employees, Interface, the world's largest producer of commercial carpeting, projects a savings of more than $35 million by the end of 1997 (see Chapter 9).

The changes required to make and market environmentally sensitive products enhance employee morale and productivity with a payoff in improved customer relations and overall returns on investment. Enhanced corporate imagery ensues, and this can help attract investors and top talent.

Competitive Advantage

Many marketers now know that being the first to the shelf with an environmental innovation brings competitive advantage. Since the first edition of *Green Marketing* was published in 1993, Rayovac introduced Renewal brand reusable alkaline batteries and redefined the market for rechargeables. With 50 percent of the production capacity for phosphate detergents, German-based Henkel pioneered the market for zeolites and claimed market leadership when their consumers shifted to phosphate-free detergents. Philips Lighting, inventors of compact fluorescent lighting technology, stood ready when businesses and electric power utilities came calling for replacements for energy-guzzling incandescents. Wellman, Inc., has expanded its business definition from plastics recycler to pioneer in the market for branded polyester fiber made from used Coke bottles.

Many of these leaders are being showered with any number of eco-accolades now offered by industry, media, government, or environmental groups. One example is the Special Edison Award for Environmental Achievement bestowed by the American Marketing Association. It has been won by Fortune 1000 firms including 3M and Procter & Gamble as well as by a raft of up-and-coming firms with a deep-green orientation, such as Natural Cotton Colours, Patagonia, and Tom's of Maine (see Exhibit 1.5).

Young, aggressive competitors adept at capturing the imaginations and winning the hearts of highly desirable environmentally and socially conscious customers are introducing some of the most exciting green products. The success of Patagonia outerwear, Stonyfield Farm yogurt, and Tom's of Maine toothpaste suggests that consumers now have higher expectations for the products they buy and that quality is an image that no longer stands apart from environmental impact.

Looking to cash in on the potential for future green-oriented sales, well-established mass marketers now shop for green companies with promising green brands; recent acquisitions include Earth's Best Baby Foods (by Heinz), Murphy's Oil Soap (Colgate-Palmolive), and EarthRite Cleaning Products (Reckitt & Colman). After nearly two decades of compromising on quality—and languishing on once-dusty health-food-store shelves as a result—

Exhibit 1.5

Special Edison Awards for Environmental Achievement Winners 1991–1996

1991:   McCloskey "Clean Air" Stain, Varnish, and Sanding
      Sealer for Wood Finishing (Valspar)
      Safest Stripper (3M)
      Downy Fabric Softener Refill Pack (Procter & Gamble)

1992:   Sanyo RechargAcell Reusable Tube and Mailback
      Recycle System (GE/Sanyo)
      Renew Recycled Content Trash Bags (Webster
      Industries)
      FoxFibre Naturally Colored Cotton (Natural Cotton
      Colours, Inc.)

1993:   Deja Shoes (Deja, Inc.)
      Green Paint Line (Green Paint Co.)
      EcoSpun Fiber (Wellman, Inc.)
      Seventh Generation*

1994:   Gridcore Building Panels (Gridcore Systems International)
      Renewal Batteries (Rayovac Corp.)
      Scotch Brite Never Rust Wool Soap Pads (3M)

1995:   AFM Line of No and Low VOC Paints, Adhesives, Caulks,
      and Floor Finishes (AFM Enterprises)
      Ogallala Down (Natural Fibers Corp.)
      Citra-Solv Degreaser and Cleaner (Shadow Lake, Inc.)
      Patagonia*

1996:   Earth's Best Baby Food (Heinz)
      Trailblazer™ Paper Made from Kenaf (Vision Paper)
      ASKO Washer (ASKO)
      Tom's of Maine*
      Alternative Agricultural Research andCommercialization
      Corp. (USDA)**

*Special Corporate Award for Environmental Achievement
**Special Citation for Environmental Achievement

Source: American Marketing Association, Chicago, Illinois

today's crop of green products finally embody all that consumers demand: an opportunity to clean up the mess without having to give up price or quality. With the deepened consumer confidence in green products that results, the market becomes legitimized.

Increased Market Share

Times are tough for marketers of branded products. Brand loyalty is near all-time lows, and the percentage of Americans who feel that some brands are worth paying more for is declining.[8] In this tough competitive climate, environmental compatibility breaks ties at the shelf. Pragmatic consumers skew purchases to those products and packages that can be recycled or otherwise safely disposed of in their communities. All else being equal, the biggest group of consumers do their bit by happily switching brands—"buycotting" companies and products deemed environmentally sound and boycotting the brands of companies with disappointing environmental track records.

These growth opportunities have not been lost on such market leaders as Procter & Gamble, McDonald's, and Compaq. They offer the greenest of mainstream products and take pains to project environmentally appropriate corporate images. Pick up a bottle of Tide laundry detergent and learn how it is "phosphate-free," contains "biodegradable cleaning agents," and is packaged in a "recycled-content bottle." Check out the basic brown paper carry-out bags and speckled (recycled) napkins at McDonald's (they are now testing "Earth Shell" compostable food wraps), and buy a Compaq PC emblazoned with the ENERGY STAR energy-saving designation (see Chapter 8).

Many executives would be shocked to discover just how many consumers are aware of—and act upon—their knowledge of corporations' track records for environmental and social responsibility. In one poll conducted by the Porter Novelli public relations firm, for example, consumers were five times more apt to think that a company's record on the environment was an "important" factor in their purchasing decisions than corporate executives believed (see Exhibit 1.6).

Exhibit 1.6

Executives Underestimate the Role of Corporate Environment and Social Responsibility in Consumers' Purchasing Decisions

*Percent saying a factor is "important"
in consumer buying decisions*

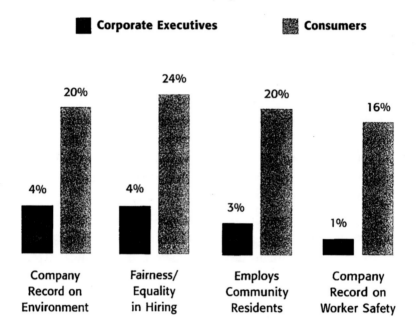

■ **Corporate Executives**   ▨ **Consumers**

24%
20%   20%
16%

4%   4%
3%
1%

| Company Record on Environment | Fairness/ Equality in Hiring | Employs Community Residents | Company Record on Worker Safety |

Source: Porter Novelli, Survey of Factors Influencing Purchasing Decisions, 1995. DDB Needham Lifestyle Survey, 1995. Chart: Adweek. Used with permission

Better Products

While much brand-switching is conducted in the name of altruism, what attracts most consumers to greener products is quite simply the prospect of higher quality: water-saving showerheads slash energy bills, concentrated laundry detergents are easier to carry and store, and nontoxic garden products are safer for children. Expect these enhanced primary benefits—of performance, convenience, price, and safety, for example, that accompany environmental improvements to continue to propel the market for environmentally preferable products in the years and decades ahead.

PERSONAL REWARDS, TOO

Green marketing offers a rare opportunity to integrate our values into the workplace. Creating products that are more in sync with nature allows us to personally contribute to environmental cleanup and helps ensure a more secure future for our children.

A mind once expanded never goes back to where it was. No longer content to promise consumers that their clothes will become "whiter than white" or that their breath is "fresher than fresh," green marketers—like their bosses who manage for a double bottom line—cultivate higher levels of satisfaction and reward. They offer their consumers the prospect of healthier, more fulfilled lives, and the power to make the world a better place. These promises and other reasons why conventional marketing is on the way out are discussed in the next chapter.

Notes

1. Roper/International Research Associates press release, 1995, p. 2.
2. "The Environmental Two-Step: Looking Back, Moving Forward," The *Times Mirror* Magazine National Environmental Forum, May 1995. Conducted by Roper Starch Worldwide, pp. 22–23.
3. "Changing Faces Stay the Same in Natural Foods," *In Business*, March/April 1996, p. 6.
4. Graham, Suzanne. "The Challenge of Selling Green," *In Business*, September/October 1995, p. 39.

5. "The Return of Roper's True-Blue Greens: Less Is More!" *Green MarketAlert*, Carl Frankel, ed., February 1994, p. 2.
6. Cushman, John H. "Critics Rise Up Against Environmental Education," *New York Times*, April 22, 1997, p. A10.
7. The ISO 14000 series of environmental quality standards is being developed under the auspices of the International Organization for Standardization, which sets voluntary standards for products and industrial practices that can be measured objectively by independent certification organizations. Based on the consensus of delegates from 111 nations, ISO 14000 would establish global rules for evaluating the environmental performance of companies and products. For more information, contact the American National Standards Institute, New York, New York.
8. Roper Reports, 96–5, p. 3

2

Consumers with a Conscience

.The notion of a "typical green consumer" continues to be elusive. Unlike discrete target groups such as Hispanic women or college-age men, green consumers are hard to define demographically. Greenness extends throughout the population to varying degrees, and green concerns are extremely diverse, encompassing a wide range of issues from global climate change and gritty smokestacks, to graffiti and lawn-mower noise on Sunday mornings.

However, research into recent buyers of green products and empirical evidence suggests that the consumers most receptive to environmentally oriented marketing appeals are educated women, 30–44, with $30,000-plus household incomes (see Exhibit 2.1). They are motivated by a desire to keep their loved ones free from harm and to make sure their children's future is secure. Influential in their community, they rally support for local environmental clubs and social causes. Their buying power and their potential to influence their peers make them a highly desirable marketing target.

That women are in the forefront of green purchasing cannot be underestimated. They do most of the shopping and although it sounds sexist, they may naturally exhibit a maternal consideration for the health and welfare of the next generation. Poll after poll shows that women place a higher importance on environmental and social purchasing criteria than men. This may reflect differences in feelings of vulnerability and control between the sexes, leading men to feel relatively less threatened by environmental ills. However, not all green consumers are as "deep green" or as active as the women discussed here—there is a host of more passive green consumers as well.

MANY SHADES OF GREEN

In conventional marketing, demographics are often a key determinant of intent to buy specific products. But in green marketing, what seems to determine willingness to purchase environmentally conscious products—more than demographics or even levels of concern for a specific environmental issue—are the consumers' feelings of being able to act on these issues, or *empowerment*.[1]

After all, consumers may be concerned about a specific issue, such as fumes emanating from the local power plant or protecting a local wildlife sanctuary, and may have the time or money to act—but if they do not believe they can make a difference, they will likely not act.

Research has corroborated that the most accurate predictor of an individual's willingness to pay a premium for renewable energy is not education or income, but membership in—or prior contributions to—environmental groups. Supporters of such utility "green pricing" programs are "surprisingly diverse, including both urban professionals and rural families."[2]

Levels of concern and feelings of empowerment, not surprisingly, vary among the population. A segmentation of consumers isolated by Roper ranges from a 15 percent core of educated, upscale individuals who say they are willing to pay a premium or forego certain conveniences to ensure a cleaner environment, to 37 percent of the public who are doggedly non-environmentalist, characterized more by indifference than by anti-environmentalist

Exhibit 2.1

Demographic Profile of Green Product Purchasers

Percent of People Who Ever Bought a Product
Because the Advertising or the Label Said the
Product Was Environmentally Safe or Biodegradable

	Yes, in past 2 months	Yes, but not in past 2 months	No, have not bought	Don't know
Sex				
Total	26	19	49	6
M	22	18	53	7
F	29	20	46	5
Age				
18–29	23	19	51	6
30–44	31	18	47	3
45–59	27	21	46	6
60+	18	18	55	8
Household Income				
Under $15,000	19	13	61	7
$15,000–$30,000	21	17	55	6
$30,000–$50,000	28	22	45	5
$50,000 +	35	22	40	4
$75,000+	34	25	38	3
Education				
Non–High School Grad	14	18	60	8
High School Grad	24	17	55	5
Some College	31	25	41	4
College Grad	33	18	42	8
Occupation				
Exec./Professional	38	16	42	4
White Collar	28	23	43	6
Blue Collar	22	22	51	5
Other Demo				
Parent of Kids 0–17	31	19	46	4
Household with Personal Computer	36	21	40	4

Source: Roper Starch Worldwide, Green Gauge, 1996. Used with permission

leanings. The in-betweeners are more or less pro-environmental—
they label themselves "environmentalists" when pollsters ask, but
for various reasons are not fully acting on their concerns (see
Exhibit 2.2).

Roper has tracked these segments of consumers since 1990. As
of 1996, the five segments, which have exhibited only modest movement overall since first identified, break out as in the following
table:

	1990	1996	
True-Blue Greens	11%	10%	{ Active
Greenback Greens	11%	5%	environmentalists
Sprouts	26%	33%	Swing group
Grousers	24%	15%	{ Not active
Basic Browns	28%	37%	environmentalists

*Source: Roper Starch Worldwide, Green Gauge, 1996. Used with
permission*

True-Blues

This 10 percent of the population hold strong environmental beliefs
and live them. The most ardent of environmentalists, they believe
they can personally make a difference in curing environmental ills.
Politically and socially active, they dedicate time and energy to environmentally safe practices themselves and attempt to influence
others to do the same. True-Blues are six times more apt to contribute money to environmental groups and over four times more
likely to shun products made by companies that are not environmentally responsible. Among the most educated of the five groups,
these people are likely to be white females living in the Midwest

or South. Almost one-third of them hold executive or professional jobs.

Greenbacks

Greenbacks, representing just 5 percent of the U.S. population, are so named because of their willingness to pay extra for environmentally preferable products. They make up that small group of consumers who say they will pay up to 22 percent more for green. They worry about the environment and support environmentalism, yet feel too busy to change their lifestyles. Although Greenbacks are generally not politically active, they are happy and eager to express their beliefs with their wallets; green purchasing within this group is very high.

Like the True-Blues, they are more likely than the average American to purchase any number of green products, such as environmentally preferable cleaning products, and products and packages made from recycled material or that can be refilled. Moreover, at 22 percent, they are twice as likely as the average American to avoid buying products from companies they perceive as environmentally irresponsible. Greenbacks are likely to be married white males living in the Midwest (35 percent) and West (24 percent). They are well educated, young (median age 37), and more likely than any of the other groups to hold white-collar jobs.

Sprouts

One-third of the U.S. population is classified as Sprouts. They are willing to engage in environmental activities from time to time but only when it requires little effort. Thus, recycling, which is curbside in many communities, is their main green activity. They read labels for greenness—although less often than the True-Blues and Greenbacks. Their greenness ends at the supermarket checkout: even though Sprouts and Greenbacks have similar median incomes, Sprouts generally won't choose a green product if it is more expensive than others on the shelf. When they do, they are only willing

Exhibit 2.2

Demographic Composition of the Five Environmental Segments

	Total Public %	True-Blue Greens %	Greenback Greens %	Sprouts %	Grousers %	Basic Browns %
Sex						
Male	48	46	63	44	46	52
Female	52	57	37	56	54	48
Median Age	42	42	37	43	42	42
Median Income	$28,000	$33,000	$33,000	$33,000	$28,000	$22,000
Education						
Less than HS	18	10	10	13	18	27
HS Grad	36	30	21	32	41	40
Some College	23	29	26	28	22	17
College Grad	22	29	44	26	19	15
Occupation						
Exec./Professional	19	29	31	24	12	14
White Collar	18	20	25	18	21	16
Blue Collar	25	19	30	24	26	27
Marital Status						
Married	58	66	67	62	58	52
Single	42	34	33	37	42	48

	Total Public %	True-Blue Greens %	Greenback Greens %	Sprouts %	Grousers %	Basic Browns %
Political/Social Ideology						
Conservative	39	31	24	39	42	40
Middle-of-the-Road	37	36	44	36	34	39
Liberal	20	29	28	20	21	16
Region						
Northeast	20	22	19	21	23	18
Midwest	23	29	35	23	24	20
South	35	27	22	30	40	43
West	21	22	24	26	13	19
Race						
White	84	91	92	90	78	79
Black	12	4	5	6	20	17
Asian	2	1	2	2	1	2
Other	2	2	1	3	1	2

Source: Roper Starch Worldwide, Green Gauge, 1996. Used with permission

Exhibit 2.3

Consumer Behavior to Protect the Environment, by Segment

Percent who do on a regular basis (1996)	Total Public %	True-Blue Greens %	Greenback Greens %	Sprouts %	Grousers %	Basic Browns %
Recycling						
Bottles, cans, glass	51	78	65	74	45	22
Newspapers	46	77	52	70	39	16
Market Behavior						
Use biodegradable soaps, detergents	22	60	27	36	13	2
Avoid buying aerosol products	20	50	30	31	15	1
Read labels to see if contents are environmentally safe	19	63	28	25	14	1
Buy products made or packaged in recycled materials	18	55	32	23	16	3
Buy products in packages that can be refilled	16	40	32	18	18	3

	Total Public %	True-Blue Greens %	Greenback Greens %	Sprouts %	Grousers %	Basic Browns %
Market Behavior *continued*						
Avoid buying products from companies who aren't environmentally responsible	11	48	22	9	8	1
Avoid restaurants using styrofoam	8	44	15	4	4	1
Other Behavior						
Take hazardous waste to collection site	22	51	32	31	17	6
Compost yard waste	17	46	32	22	15	3
Take own bags to supermarket	10	36	9	11	11	1
Cut down on car use	6	24	8	5	4	1
Contribute money to environmental causes	5	31	9	2	3	1
Volunteer for an environmental group	4	18	1	3	5	less than 1
Write to politicians	3	26	2	less than 1	less than 1	less than 1

Source: Roper Starch Worldwide, Green Gauge, 1996. Used with permission

to pay up to 4 percent extra. More than half (56 percent) are female and at 43, they have the highest median age among the five groups. Sprouts are distributed evenly across the country. They are well educated, and just under two-thirds of them are married. They comprise the swing group that can go either way on any environmental issue. With more education, they are often the source for new Greenbacks and True-Blues.

Grousers

Fifteen percent of the U.S. population are Grousers. These people do not believe that individuals play any significant part in protecting the environment. Instead, they feel that the responsibility belongs to the government and large corporations. Often confused and uninformed about environmental problems, 45 percent of Grousers recycle bottles and cans regularly, but grudgingly; they do so to comply with local laws rather than to contribute to a better environment. They are far more likely than any other group, including the Basic Browns, to use excuses to rationalize their lax environmental behavior. True to their name, Grousers complain that they are too busy, that it is hard to get involved, that green products cost too much and don't work as well, and, finally, that everything they do will be inconsequential in the whole scheme of things. Their overall attitude is that it is someone else's problem, so why bother. Demographically, Grousers are similar to the national average, although with a somewhat higher proportion of African-American members.

Basic Browns

Representing 37 percent of the population, Basic Browns are not tuned in or turned on to the environment. They are simply not convinced that environmental problems are all that serious. Basic Browns do not make excuses for their inactivity; they just don't care. The indifference of this group makes them less than half as likely as the average American to recycle and only 1 percent boycott products for environmental reasons as opposed to the 11 percent national average. Three percent buy recycled goods compared to 18 percent nationally. The largest of the five groups, Basic Browns have the lowest median income, the lowest level of education, and live disproportionately in the South. For the Basic Browns, there are just too many other things to worry about.

As noted in Exhibit 2.3, environmental behavior varies significantly across these segments, suggesting that not all categories of products or individual brands are affected equally by consumers' environmental concerns. A close look at the behavior of the most active segment, the True-Blues, demonstrates the relative depth of their commitment. Given their societal influence, this suggests the types of behavior that can be expected from a much bigger group of consumers in the future. More than half of the True-Blues return glass bottles, look for green messages on packages, recycle newspapers, and do the laundry with "biodegradable" detergents. As social and style leaders, their forceful presence can be expected to exert increasing pressure, particularly on the Greenbacks and the Sprouts—underscoring the opportunities of marketers who can win over these influential True-Blues.

Three Deep-Green Sub-Segments

Not all deep-green activists are alike. It is possible to further segment them into three groups mirroring the major types of environmental issues and causes: Planet Passionates, Health Fanatics, and Animal Lovers.

With the goals of protecting wildlife and keeping the environment pristine for recreational purposes, Planet Passionates focus on issues relating to land, air, and water. They recycle bottles and cans, avoid overpackaged products, clean up bays and rivers, and boycott tropical hardwood.

As implied by their name, Health Fanatics focus on the health consequences of environmental problems. They worry about getting cancer from too much exposure to the sun, genetic defects

Exhibit 2.4
Segmentation by Consumer Motives

Planet Passionates	Health Fanatics	Animal Lovers
Likely to belong to:	*Likely to belong to:*	*Likely to belong to:*
Sierra Club	Americans for Safe Food	Greenpeace
Natural Resources Defense Council	Mothers and Others Against Pesticides	World Wildlife Fund
American Rivers	National Coalition Against the	National Audubon Society
Rainforest Alliance	Misuse of Pesticides	Humane Society
Friends of the Earth		PETA
Likely environmental behavior:	*Likely environmental behavior:*	*Likely environmental behavior:*
Conserve energy, water	Buy organic foods and bottled water	Boycott tuna, ivory
Recycle bottles, cans	Use sunscreens	Buy "cruelty-free" cosmetics
Buy recycled paper	Buy unbleached coffee filters	Avoid fur
Avoid excessive packaging	Read *Organic Gardening,*	Boycott Exxon
Read *Sierra* Magazine and *Amicus Journal*	*Prevention,* and *Delicious*	Read *Animal Agenda* and *Audubon*

Source: J. Ottman Consulting, Inc.

from radiation and toxic waste, and the long-term impact on their children's health of pesticides on fruit. Health Fanatics frequent natural-food stores, buy bottled water, and eat organic foods.

Animal Lovers, the third major group of deep greens, protect animal rights. They boycott tuna and fur, and their favorite causes include manatees and spotted owls. Animal Lovers check to see if products are "cruelty-free." They are likely to be vegetarians.

GREEN CONSUMER PSYCHOLOGY AND BUYING STRATEGIES

Although they express their environmental concerns in individual ways, green consumers are motivated by universal needs (see Exhibit 2.5). These needs translate into new purchasing strategies with implications for the way products are developed and marketed.

NEED FOR CONTROL

Green consumers put familiar products under a magnifying glass of environmental scrutiny, and their buzzwords signifying envi-

---

Exhibit 2.5
Green Consumer Psychology and Buying Strategies

Needs	*Strategies*
Information ⟶	Read Labels
Control ⟶	Take preventive measures
Make a difference/alleviate guilt ⟶	Switch brands
Maintain lifestyles ⟶	Buy interchangeable alternatives

Source: J. Ottman Consulting, Inc.

---

ronmental compatibility abound. Starting in the late 1980s, such terms as "recyclable," "biodegradable," and "environmentally friendly" made cash registers ring throughout upper-middle-class neighborhoods from coast to coast. As we approach the millennium, "sustainable," "compostable," and "bio-based" are being added to the list.

As shown in Exhibit 2.6, the broad scope of these buzzwords suggests that green consumers scrutinize products at every phase of their life cycle, from raw material procurement, manufacturing, and production straight through to product reuse, repair, recycling, or eventual disposal. While in-use attributes continue to be of primary importance, environmental shopping agendas now increasingly encompass factors consumers can't feel or see. They want to know how raw materials are procured and where they come from, how food is grown, and what their potential impact is on the environment once they land in the trash bin.

As a second control strategy, green consumers patronize manufacturers and retailers they trust, and boycott the wares of suspected polluters. In the absence of complete knowledge about a product's environmental characteristics, purchasing from upright manufacturers and retailers provides an added layer of assurance that products are safe.

At 11 percent, a near-record number of consumers boycott brands of companies with poor environmental track records (see Exhibit 2.3). Apple growers well remember the boycott waged in 1989 by mothers who feared the long-term effects of the Alar pesticide on their children's health. In 1995, to protest French nuclear tests in the Pacific, wine drinkers targeted the 25 million–30 million bottle harvest of Beaujolais. The market for Beaujolais "all but collapsed" in Japan, the Netherlands, and Scandinavia, and "disappeared" in Australia and New Zealand close to the testing.[3]

As a final control strategy, a small but growing number of consumers now search for simpler ways of living. In 1991, researchers for the *Yankelovich Monitor* reported on a long-term trend that

Exhibit 2.6
Green Purchasing Buzzwords

Raw Materials

Sustainably harvested
Petroleum-free
Plant-based

Manufacturing/ Production

Non-polluting
Unbleached
Pesticide-free

Packaging

Recycled
Non-aerosol
Source-reduced

Distribution

Energy-efficient
Reusable packaging

Marketing

Ethical
Informative
Cause-related

In-Use

Low-fume
Resource-efficient
Durable

After-Use

Recyclable
Refillable
Reusable

Manufacturer

Socially responsible
CERES signator

Source: J. Ottman Consulting, Inc.

showed new products, the lifeblood of marketers, were losing appeal. They attributed this to two factors—a growing dislike for shopping in general and the perception that "new" is risky.[4] For proof, consider what's happening to women's shopping habits.

The *New York Times* reports that women's apparel sales are on a long-term slide (from a record $84 billion in 1989 to $73 billion in 1995), despite a 37 percent gain in overall personal spending during the same period. Apparently, women are deciding there are better ways to spend their money than shopping. Picking up the slack are "other passions, from one's children to investing, to a variety of goods and services being marketed as salves for a stressful life: backpacking trips and gardening tools, vanilla-scented candles, spiritual retreats, and manicures."[5]

Women are not the only ones tired of the "live-to-work, work-to-consume" rat race. A nationwide survey conducted for the Merck Family Fund shows that most Americans are concerned about materialistic values and the impact of indulgent consumption on our environment. According to the poll, 82 percent of Americans agree that "Most of us buy and consume far more than we need." Suggesting that consumers intuitively understand that today's lifestyles are unsustainable, 58 percent say it would make a "big difference" in helping the environment "if we taught our children to be less materialistic."[6] Attempting to reconcile values centered on family, responsibility, and community, more than a quarter said that "in the past five years, they had voluntarily made changes in their life which resulted in making less money in order to have a more balanced life." When asked what would make them happier, two-thirds said they wanted to spend more time with family and friends.

The mass consumer is still ambivalent about how to reconcile personal values with present consumption modes. However, a small but growing number of consumers address their needs to protect the environment, enhance spirituality, reduce stress, and build long-term financial security with strategies such as avoiding unnecessary purchases; buying high-quality, durable products; and using products that do several jobs. Representing a movement called Voluntary Simplicity, these lean consumers accounted for 4 percent of all Baby Boomers as of 1994, and are projected to represent 15 percent by the year 2000.[7]

Not to be confused with the back-to-basics crowd of the early 1970s, this small but growing contingent of upscale, educated adults do not reject consumption out of hand; some have secondhand BMWS in the driveway and designer clothes among their pared-down and largely monochromatic (black/white/gray) wardrobes. They happily trade in high-powered jobs and the hefty incomes they provide to spend additional time with loved ones, appreciate nature, and pursue creative activities. Expect their ways to depress sales of new homes, convenience foods, and second cars, while at the same time accelerating momentum in natural foods, easy-to-care-for clothes in classic styles, travel, and other leisure pursuits.

 Ca/e /tud-y   **Profile of a Simplifier**

Kathy Bryant was living the American Dream. As an editor, writer, and photographer for Duke Power in Charlotte, North Carolina, her career was in the fast lane. But a key element was missing from her life.

In 1988 when her father died, Kathy realized she was too far from her home and family in College Park, Maryland—a town her great-grandfather had founded.

She called her uncle, a career utility executive, for advice. He urged her to "get off the phone and tell your boss you are quitting." She did.

A week before moving home she received an offer for freelance work. With her mother's support, Kathy restructured her life and work. As a freelancer, she controls when and for whom she works. She loves the variety of jobs she has done—including photographing Al Gore and Queen Elizabeth—opportunities she would never have had otherwise. And her mother benefits, too. Kathy provides companionship, helps care for the house, and encourages her mother to be active. Her mother is no longer lonely but thrives on the activity.

"I am really happy since I moved home. I cherish the time with my mother, the time in my garden. I can garden all day if I want," says Kathy. Managing her time required some discipline, she notes, as did learning to tailor her spending needs to her new income.

Kathy thinks in terms of life and happiness, not in terms of money and career. She has learned to live with less by eliminating small items like magazine subscriptions. When considering a purchase, she thinks about the articles she needs to write to pay for it. Being more deliberate about her purchases makes her spending "more real."

"'Too much of our 'throw-away society' is based on creating and consuming," says Kathy. "Leading an alternative lifestyle demonstrates that you can consume less and have a very good life."

Kathy defines herself in terms of life choices, not career choices. She values the opportunity to create her own life. She looks for fun ways to make money, and volunteers with local organizations.

The quality of Kathy's life has increased dramatically, as has the quality of her work. "This is," admits Kathy, "the golden period of my life." She has found the vital ingredients previously absent— self-respect, self-definition, and satisfaction. That is Kathy Bryant's equation for fulfillment.[8]

A final control strategy relates to health and is best depicted in the revolution now underway called "clean food." Described as "a new standard for health and reliability," clean foods are "free of artificial preservatives, coloring, irradiation, synthetic pesticides, fungicides, rodenticides, ripening agents, fumigants, drug residues, and growth hormones," and exclude those foods that are "processed, packaged, transported, and stored to retain maximum nutritional value."

Motivated in part by lack of trust in government's ability to keep food pure, the appeal of clean foods has fueled escalating sales for organic produce, bottled water, health-food supermarkets, alternative medical treatments, and dietary supplements.[9]

Clean food and organic food provide irresistible aesthetic and spiritual benefits as well. According to Alice Waters, one of the first chefs to stress the importance of locally grown organic food for its taste and environmental preferability, "It's also a connection with the kind of food that is alive, fresh, seasonal, and a connection with the people who are growing it. A deep and lasting sensual connection is made, and once you eat food like that, you can't turn back."[10]

Keep an eye on this trend. Now representing a small (3 percent) portion of the population of those most concerned about food and its relation to health, it could engage up to 30 percent of the population in the next 20 years by one analyst's estimate.[11]

NEED TO MAKE A DIFFERENCE

Reflecting a deeply felt need of Baby Boomers to assume responsibility for their actions, green consumers want to feel that they can, at least in some small way, make a difference. It is no coincidence that they respond to such empowering promises as those represented by the bestseller, *50 Simple Things You Can Do to Save the Earth*. This need stems as much from a desire for control, as it does from the corresponding need to alleviate guilt.

Consumers feel especially guilty about environmental ills they can do something about, but do not. They readily acknowledge the role of their own consumption in despoiling the environment (see Exhibit 2.7), and while they feel they have improved slightly since the early 1990s, they rate themselves as just a little better than large

Exhibit 2.7

Root Causes of Environmental Problems

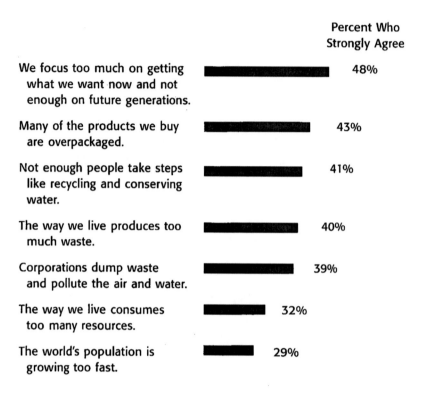

Percent Who
Strongly Agree

We focus too much on getting
what we want now and not
enough on future generations. — 48%

Many of the products we buy
are overpackaged. — 43%

Not enough people take steps
like recycling and conserving
water. — 41%

The way we live produces too
much waste. — 40%

Corporations dump waste
and pollute the air and water. — 39%

The way we live consumes
too many resources. — 32%

The world's population is
growing too fast. — 29%

Source: "Yearning for Balance." A nationwide survey conducted by the Harwood Group from February 20 to March 1, 1995. Sponsored by the Merck Family Fund. Used with permission

businesses when asked "Who's Dragging Their Feet on Environmental Protection?" (see Exhibit 2.8). They see themselves as being able to do little to fix serious problems like global climate change or ozone layer depletion. However, they do feel a responsibility to cut down on excess packaging and take steps like recycling and conserving water.

Everyday behavior, such as disposing of what is perceived as excessive packaging or keeping the water running while shaving, can serve as daily reminders of personal environmental transgres-

Exhibit 2.8
"Who's Doing a Good Job on the Environment?"

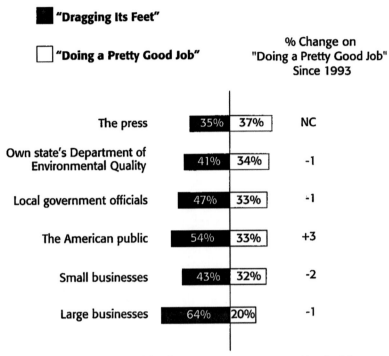

■ "Dragging Its Feet"

☐ "Doing a Pretty Good Job"

% Change on
"Doing a Pretty Good Job"
Since 1993

	"Dragging Its Feet"	"Doing a Pretty Good Job"	% Change
The press	35%	37%	NC
Own state's Department of Environmental Quality	41%	34%	-1
Local government officials	47%	33%	-1
The American public	54%	33%	+3
Small businesses	43%	32%	-2
Large businesses	64%	20%	-1

Source: Roper Starch Worldwide, Green Gauge, 1996. Used with permission

sions. Use of products that are, rightly or wrongly, associated with environmental blight—disposable diapers, plastic-foam cups, and aerosol spray cans—reinforces their guilt.

Consumers' desire to alleviate guilt manifests itself in indirect ways. New mothers may continue to use Pampers knowing they will wind up in a landfill. However, to compensate, they may go out of their way to recycle the family's bottles, cans, and newspapers to help offset the space in the landfill taken up by the diaper. This compensatory behavior suggests that each consumer has a unique repertoire of activities and trade-offs he or she is willing to make to help out the planet. One's environmental repertoire likely reflects such factors as age, lifestyle, income, and particular environmental interests and concerns, as well as geographic location, including access to recycling and other after-use or disposal options. Consumers' feelings of guilt and eco-inadequacy have not been assuaged since the early 1990s; a lengthening list of environmentally driven activities and purchasing continues to fill the gaps.

Green consumers are, by definition, very sincere in their intentions. As much as they are willing to do today, as their knowledge and commitment grows, they become more aware of what else they can do. The gap between what they feel they should be doing and what they are actually doing makes them feel guilty and sometimes defensive. Purchasing green products and taking measures around the house give environmentally concerned consumers a psychic lift by helping them align their beliefs with their actions.

For instance, anecdotal evidence suggests that consumers feel positively reinforced by recycling (typically one of their first steps down the path to green). Once engaged, they start asking, "What else can I do?" The significantly high levels of recycling that now occur may provide one explanation for the current rebound in green-product purchasing.

NEED FOR INFORMATION

Consumers heading off to supermarkets and health-food stores in search of greener goods need to know how to tell the "green" products from the "brown" ones, which stores or catalogs to find them in, and how to spot the products and packages that can be recycled in their community. Their task is tricky.

Such environmentally preferable products as mercury-free alkaline batteries or paper towels made from recycled content are often indistinguishable from "brown" ones. Some green products with as yet limited appeal like low-flow showerheads and citrus-based cleaning products are often tucked away in health-food shops and direct-mail catalogs beyond the reach of mainstream shoppers. Such alternative cleaning products as baking soda and white vinegar are easily found in supermarkets but are not necessarily labeled as "green."

Products representing new and unfamiliar technologies are constantly being launched onto supermarket shelves. Consumers' understanding of environmental issues is growing but continues to be low—only 8 percent of consumers claim to know a lot about environmental issues.[12] So even the most environmentally enthused consumers need to be educated on why some types of products represent less environmental harm than others. Providing such information and education still provides the biggest opportunity to expand the market to mainstream consumers.

Information aimed at filling in consumers' knowledge gaps is now in plentiful supply. Sources include manufacturers; packaging; advertising; consumer media, including several green shopping sites on the World Wide Web; and the specialty environmental press composed of consumer-oriented magazines, including *E*, *Mother Jones*, and *Utne Reader,* as well as such advocacy group publications as *Sierra, Audubon, World Watch,* and *Amicus Journal.* Although much of the information is more consistent and less confusing than its late 1980s counterparts, a profusion of labels, claims, eco-seals, and images on products and packaging, as well as inconsistent media stories, often confuse and frustrate consumers who are just beginning to give green products another try.

Win consumers over by educating them with clear, consistent information about the environmental issues associated with your products.

NEED TO MAINTAIN LIFESTYLE

Although a small number of highly committed consumers will sacrifice in the name of altruism, the great majority of consumers, understandably, are still not prepared to give up such coveted product attributes as performance, quality, convenience, or price. Product efficacy continues to strongly influence consumer purchase decisions. As too many green marketers learned the hard way, environmentally preferable products must be priced competitively or project superior primary benefits in order to attract a wide market.

For the great many working women—and working mothers in particular—short-term, immediate concerns like getting through the day often preempt longer-term and more remote environmental goals. Greened up versions of major products such as super-concentrated laundry detergents available at local supermarkets meet their needs and sell well as a result. Consumers want the products they buy to be delivered in a safe, sanitary, and attractive manner. Their desire to buy products with minimal packaging conflicts with their greater needs for safety (*e.g.*, tamperproof lids) and convenience (*e.g.*, microwavable food).

Historically, how food looks determined its appetite appeal and perceived purity. This is slowly changing, due largely to education efforts on the part of organic growers and more effective distribution methods. Fewer consumers now need to choose between organically grown apples with an inconsistent appearance and perfect-looking apples ripened with chemical agents.

Resistance to paying a premium will not go away any time soon. Many consumers simply cannot afford to pay extra for any type of product, green or not; today's consumers are especially spoiled by everyday low-pricing strategies and mass-merchandiser discounting. Although wallets are gradually opening wider for green goods as a result of increased education, most consumers are still not willing to pay extra money upfront for products that promise a long-term payback, such as energy-efficient refrigerators or lightbulbs.

The inconsistent or even downright poor quality of green products offered in days gone by—low-flow showerheads that sputtered and green-hued fluorescent lighting that flickered, for example— seems to have given their modern-day successors a bad name. Happily, most of today's green products adeptly combine performance with environmental quality. Now that they can have their cake and eat it too, expect mainstream consumers to drop more green products into their shopping carts in the years ahead.

In the past, premium pricing and vaguely worded environmental claims made consumers suspect manufacturers of price gouging. If products are smaller, more compact, or simpler looking than their "brown" counterparts, consumers intuitively believe they should cost less, not more. But this is slowly changing. For example, a small but growing number of consumers seek out products and packaging that have been "source reduced." This is particularly true in the 1,800 or so U.S. municipalities that have volume-based, "pay as you throw" household waste-disposal fees, where consumers are typically charged for each bag of waste they drop at the curb.

Historical reluctance to pay a premium for green goods seems to be softening as consumers connect environmental responsibility with health or other direct benefits. Sales of organically grown "clean" foods, natural cosmetics, and cottons grown without pesticides demonstrate that when it comes to green products, the greater the self-interest, the greater the perceived threat, the greater the willingness to pay. The small but growing Voluntary Simplifier movement suggests that some consumers will even go so far as to change jobs or rearrange their lifestyle altogether if the rewards of more time and a richer life are present.

The success stories of the many marketers who are developing greener products that balance consumers' primary needs with environmental responsibility are told in the next chapter.

Notes

1. This is also referred to as "perceived consumer effectiveness" in "Green Consumers in the 1990s: Profile and Implications for Advertising," James A. Roberts, Baylor University, *Journal of Business Research*, Volume 36, p. 226.

2. Baugh, Keith, Brian Byrnes, Clive Jones, and Maribeth Rahimzadeh, "Green Pricing: Removing the Guesswork," *Public Utilities Fortnightly*, August 1995, p. 27.

3. Whitney, Craig R., "Nuclear Tests Cutting Sales of Beaujolais," *New York Times*, November 17, 1995, p. A10.

4. Hayward, Susan, of Yankelovich, Clancy, and Shulman, presentation to the American Marketing Association's "Environmental Conference: Green Marketing from a Marketer's Perspective," October 1991.

5. Steinhauer, Jennifer, and Constance C. R. White, "Women's New Relationship with Fashion," *New York Times*, August 5, 1996, p. D9.

6. "Yearning for Balance: Views of Americans on Consumption, Materialism, and the Environment," prepared for the Merck Family Fund by the Harwood Group, Bethesda, Maryland, July 1995.

7. Valdes, Alisa, "Living Simply. '90s Style Means Earning Less to Enjoy Life More," *Boston Globe*, September 1, 1994, p. A3.

8. Barry, Sam, "Kathy Bryant Profile," *Co-op America Quarterly*, Number 37, Summer 1995, p. 22.

9. Burros, Marian, "A New Goal Beyond Organic: Clean Food," *New York Times*, February 7, 1996, p. C1.

10. *Ibid.*, p. C4.

11. *Ibid.*, p. C4.

12. Roper Starch Worldwide, Green Gauge, 1995.

3

Why Conventional Marketing Won't Work

Conventional marketing is out. Green marketing is in. Effectively addressing the needs of consumers with a raised environmental consciousness cannot be achieved with the same assumptions and formulas that guided consumer marketing in the high production–high consumption postwar era. New strategies and innovative product and service offerings are required.

Conventional marketing entails developing products that meet consumers' needs at affordable prices and then communicating the benefits of those products in a compelling way. Environmental marketing is more complex. It serves two key objectives:

- to develop products that balance consumers' needs for quality, performance, affordable pricing, and convenience with *environmental compatibility*, that is, minimal impact on the environment

- to project an image of high quality, including *environmental sensitivity*, relating to both a product's attributes and its manufacturer's track record for environmental achievement

These objectives cannot be met using conventional marketing strategies. Marketers in the age of environmental consumerism face tough new standards. Environmental consumerism represents deep psychological and sociological shifts, as did its predecessors—Naderism and feminism. Naderism spurred marketers to produce safer, higher-quality products and to advertise those products with more credible claims. Feminism forced marketers to develop convenient products and to portray women with a new respect. Meeting the challenges of environmental consumerism presents its own mandates for corporate processes, product quality, and promotion.

To realize that conventional strategies won't succeed, one need only recall the unsavory backlash that pioneering green marketers incurred over what was perceived by environmentalists, regulators, and the press as inconsistent and often misleading labels and claims. Marketers, desirous of keeping in step with competitors and encouraged by polls erroneously suggesting that overwhelming majorities of consumers would pay hefty premiums for greener goods, rushed headlong to underscore the environmental benefits of their offerings, however insignificant or coincidental. Indeed, according to J. Walter Thompson Company, green claims quadrupled between 1989 and 1990. Trash bags and diapers were touted as "degradable" and hair sprays were branded as "ozone friendly." One product label even claimed "earth friendly since 1889."

The resulting deluge of skepticism, confusion, and regulatory nightmares that these green claims spawned quickly proved that environmental marketing involves more than tweaking one or two product attributes and dressing up packages with meaningless (and often misleading) claims. Too many marketers learned the hard way that partaking of environmentally related opportunities requires a total corporate commitment to greening one's products and communications. It affects how a corporation interacts with all the groups and individuals who may be affected by its environmental practices. As such, this commitment needs to be founded on a thorough greening of one's entire company—and values.

The New Marketing Paradigm

A new paradigm is now in the making. Basic assumptions about how best to cater to consumer needs are in question. Successful green marketers no longer view consumers as individuals with insatiable appetites for material goods, but as human beings concerned about the condition of the world around them, how they themselves interact with the rest of nature, and cognizant of how material goods impact their lives positively as well as negatively, short term as well as long term.

Products are no longer designed in a linear "cradle-to-grave" fashion, with no regard for the long-term impact on society of their eventual disposal or no appreciation for the value of natural resources they represent. A "one-size-fits-all" system of nationally marketed brands now gives way to more flexible product offerings that best fit regional environmental considerations. Yesterday's resource-intensive products are being replaced by innovative products with radical new designs, even with "dematerialized services." These offerings are marketed with ads and promotions that derive added value from the educational messages they impart and the values they project.

The corporations that excel at green marketing are those that are pro-active in nature. Aiming to surpass minimal compliance standards, they define the rules by which they and their competitors will be judged. Ecologically responsive corporations consider themselves to be like nature's processes—interdependent. These corporations join with corporate environmental stakeholders in cooperative, positive alliances, and they work hand in hand with suppliers and retailers to manage environmental issues throughout the value chain. Internally, crossfunctional teams convene to find the best possible holistic solutions to environmental challenges. Long-term rather than short-term in their orientation, these companies manage with a double bottom line—one bottom line for profits, the other one reflecting their contribution to society.

Exhibit 3.1
The New Green Marketing Paradigm

	Conventional Marketing	Green Marketing
Consumers	Consumers with lifestyles	Human beings with lives*
Products	"Cradle-to-grave"	"Cradle-to-cradle"
	One-size-fits-all	Flexible
	Products	Services
Marketing and Communications	Selling-oriented	Educational
	End benefits	Values
Corporate	Reactive	Pro-active
	Independent	Interdependent
	Competitive	Cooperative
	Departmentalized	Holistic
	Short-term oriented	Long-term oriented
	Profit-maximizing	Double bottom line

William McDonough
Source: J. Ottman Consulting, Inc.

THE SEVEN STRATEGIES OF GREEN MARKETING SUCCESS

The currency of the green business world is innovation, flexibility, change, and heart. New rules have emerged from the cloud of green marketing dust kicked up in the late 1980s and early 1990s. We know better what works—and what does not. Seven strategies that work are listed in Exhibit 3.2. Using these strategies, eco-entrepreneurs Gary Hirshberg and Samuel Kayman set a greener pace that others now must follow.

Exhibit 3.2

J. Ottman Consulting's Seven Winning Strategies of Green Marketing

1. Do your homework. Understand the full range of environmental, economic, political, and social issues that affect your consumer and your products and services now and over the long term.

2. Create new products and services that balance consumers' desires for high quality, convenience, and affordable pricing with minimal environmental impact over the entire life of your products.

3. Empower consumers with solutions. Help them understand the issues that affect your business as well as the benefits of your environmentally preferable technology, materials, and designs.

4. Establish credibility for your marketing efforts.

5. Build coalitions with corporate environmental stakeholders.

6. Communicate your corporate commitment and project your values.

7. Don't quit. Continuously strive for "zero" environmental impact of your products and processes; learn from your mistakes.

Source: J. Ottman Consulting, Inc.

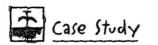 Case Study   **Stonyfield Farm Takes a Values-Based Approach**

Stonyfield Farm of Londonderry, New Hampshire, has witnessed explosive growth in its thirteen years of existence. Gary Hirshberg and Samuel Kayman, the founders of this now 125-person company, have seen their yogurt- and dairy-product-based business skyrocket from regional to national—and now international—distribution. A big reason for the company's rapid growth is the products themselves. Stonyfield's popular products represent healthy alternatives to other brands, giving them a competitive advantage in a market where more and more consumers are choosier about the food products they buy.

However, it isn't only its yogurt that sets this company apart from its competition. Stonyfield began as a school to help revitalize New England agriculture and to educate people about environmental practices and issues faced by local dairy farmers. Building upon this history of environmental education, the company makes pioneering social and environment-related business practices central to business, values, and growth. Such business practices ensure markets for the pure dairy products produced on New England farms, while teaching industry a thing or two about how to run a socially and environmentally responsible business.

Hirshberg and Kayman began making high-quality yogurt in 1983 as a way to raise money for their nonprofit school. Today, Stonyfield produces the purest, most nutritious, and best-tasting yogurt available, while supporting various socially and environmentally beneficial causes. Environmental initiatives include annual contributions to worthy environmental groups, extensive recycling programs, and ongoing customer education.

Only the Finest Will Do

Hirshberg and Kayman run their company with five objectives; the first is to "provide and sell the highest-quality agricultural products available." Stonyfield makes its premium-quality yogurt from milk supplied by dairy farms that do not use rBGH, a controversial synthetic bovine-growth hormone. The yogurt contains none of the gelatins, starches, thickeners, or other chemical additives used in most other yogurts. To further notch its products above competition, Stonyfield uses a less refined sugar and all Stonyfield products contain both *Acidophilus* and *Bifidus*, active bacterial cultures known to improve digestion, especially in children. The result: a healthier, better-tasting product appreciated by health-conscious consumers.

And the unbeatable quality pays off in unbeatable margins. Stonyfield commands a 4–5 percent price premium, while generating continued markets for local dairy farmers.

Interactive Marketing Programs

Stonyfield sells its products and values through interactive marketing programs designed to heighten customer awareness about the quality of its products and the importance of supporting local dairy farmers and other causes—the second of Stonyfield's company objectives. Getting consumers involved is key to Stonyfield's success. Consumers appreciate the company's healthful approach to production, but also like becoming empowered via the company's programs.

One such program is "Have-a-Cow," a lighthearted approach to teaching consumers about where milk comes from. Consumers can "adopt" one of the cows whose milk gets transformed into Stonyfield Farm's yogurt and ice cream. Sponsoring consumers receive a kit including a glossy cow photograph, an in-depth cow biography, and a certificate signed by Stonyfield Farm president, Gary Hirshberg. In addition, twice a year, they receive a Stonyfield Farm "Moosletter" filled with news about each cow on the farm. Notes Hirshberg on the program's goals, "We started the 'Have-a-Cow' program in 1989 as a way to help consumers stay in touch with where the food comes from. By seeing how a farm works from the point of view of a cow, consumers gain a better understanding of the importance of agriculture and the need to protect the environment." This program has already empowered 30,000 participants to feel like they are doing good by supporting Stonyfield's policies—a common theme with the company's environmental efforts.

A related "Just Say Moo" campaign educates consumers about the extensive use of the controversial rBGH hormones and their potential negative implications for family farmers. Marshaling a variety of public outreach components, this effort aims to boost awareness of sound agricultural practices and publicize Stonyfield's own stand on the issue. Billboards and radio spots urge consumers to call the company's 800 telephone number to learn about other ways to get involved.

A third campaign, dubbed "Flip Your Lid," conducted in April 1996, empowered consumers to act upon various environmental and social causes. In one phase of the program, the plastic lids on the Stonyfield Farm yogurt cups became readymade letters to Congress. One side of the lid read: "The planet is everybody's business. We all must work to ensure a healthy planet for generations to come. You can act on behalf of your children today by 'flipping your lid.'" On the underside of the lid was a letter to Congress ready to be signed and mailed, saying "Government should be more efficient, but not at the cost of a polluted planet. I don't support cuts in environmental funding for they deny our children their rights to a healthy Earth. Please vote on behalf of the environment." In addition, a toll-free number supplied information, name, and voting records in Congress. During a four-week campaign, more than 1.5 million lids reached consumers through supermarkets, natural-food stores, and college Earth Day events. Supporters of the campaign included Ben & Jerry's, Reebok, Fetzer Vineyards, the Audubon Society, Greenpeace, and the Natural Resources Defense Council.

The Lid program's other foci included the tenth anniversary of Farm Aid, the Real Goods catalog of products promoting energy independence and sustainable living, and prevention of handgun violence. In each case, one million lids were produced and distributed nationwide over a four-week period, translating into coverage for Stonyfield Farm and the specific causes, supported by word-of-mouth, lid recipients' newsletters, national TV exposure, and other forms of publicity.

Profits for the Planet

Ever-mindful of the public pulse, Stonyfield financially supports environmental and agricultural causes. Through its "Profits for the

Planet" program, the company donates 10 percent of its profits to organizations and farmers who work toward advancing sustainable agriculture. This practice demonstrates two key elements of the company. By supporting a variety of advocacy groups, Stonyfield builds upon its agricultural education base and shows a concern for environmental awareness that extends beyond the company's own marketing persona. Such support also proves that socially and environmentally responsible business enterprise is profitable.

Though many companies tout their "greenness" through environmental group donations, Stonyfield avoids what Gary Hirshberg terms "greenscamming" by instituting various in-house practices that answer to the third company objective of employee benefits and the need to "practice what you preach."

The company's full commitment to green includes such in-house practices as a company-wide recycling program, an energy-saving lighting system retrofitted in accordance with the U.S. Environmental Protection Agency's Green Lights program, and

---

Exhibit 3.3
Stonyfield Farm Yogurt Lid

Source: Stonyfield Farm. Reprinted with permission

efforts aimed at creating environmentally preferable packaging. These changes resulted from an ecological audit performed in the company's early years. Internal efforts, policies, and programs demonstrate Stonyfield Farm's commitment to being as green on the inside as it is on the outside—a fact the company demonstrates through daily plant tours.

Stonyfield's commitment has catapulted the tiny dairy upstart into the green spotlight. Health-conscious consumers all over the United States seek the benefits of Stonyfield's yogurt and appreciate the company's efforts to act in an environmentally and socially responsible way. Consumers also like Stonyfield's educational programs, which speak to their own desires for responsible behavior. Additionally, Stonyfield's customers appreciate the personal connection the company offers and the fact that Stonyfield puts profits into organizations they care about. Through its policies and programs, Stonyfield helps its consumers get involved and provides an outlet to "go green."

In addition to consumer recognition, Stonyfield Farm has also drawn considerable media attention, including the highly coveted 1994 America's Corporate Conscience Award for Environmental Stewardship from the Council on Economic Priorities, the 1991 Business Ethics Award from *Business Ethics* magazine, and the 1992 Manufacturer of the Year from *NH Business* magazine, as well as a 1993 ranking in *Inc.* magazine's "Employers of the Year."

Stonyfield's positive, values-based orientation has allowed the company to fulfill its fourth and fifth objectives—to recognize obligations to investors and serve as a model that environmentally and socially responsible companies can be profitable. In Gary Hirshberg's words, "Consumers want businesses to do the right thing, and businesses that do the right thing get rewarded for it." Stonyfield's social and environmental focus draws positive recognition, and the business benefits accordingly. Sales over the past decade at Stonyfield have grown tenfold—from $3 million in fiscal year 1990 to $31 million in fiscal year 1997. Stonyfield Farm distributes yogurt in all 50 states, as well as in Britain and Russia.

These positive results, in combination with the fulfillment of its company objectives, allow Stonyfield to present itself as a model environmentally responsible and profitable company. Gary Hirshberg sums up his company's commitment to teaching, "We have experienced the direct benefits of going the extra mile in terms of environmental advocacy, employee wellness and participation, and other socially responsible practices. Our mission is to show the largest companies on Earth that they, too, can reap such benefits. Most of the problems we face will be reversed only when businesses make the solution their priority."

4

Green by Design

Environmental product issues are varied and complex. They span every phase of a product's life cycle, and include a plethora of sub-issues, such as conservation of natural resources like water and land, energy efficiency, and protection of natural habitats and endangered species, as detailed in Exhibit 4.1.

Upgrading products and packaging to minimize environmental impact can be tricky. What may appear to be an environmental benefit may actually result in little or no added value to the environment. For example, plastic trash bags that are technically designed to disintegrate in the presence of sunlight will not degrade when buried in a landfill. Sometimes, the presumed greening of one attribute can actually increase overall environmental impact. Cpc, the makers of Mueller's pasta, found that converting to recycled carton material would actually add about 20 percent to the width of their packaging material. This would at least partially offset savings to the environment, considering the added energy needed to ship the new boxes.[1] For these reasons, and also to prevent backlash from consumers, environmental groups, and other stakeholders, all of whom may be quick to point out the shortcomings of products and packaging touted as green, a thorough approach to "greening" is required. A tool called life cycle inventory (LCI) can help.

Exhibit 4.1

Green Product Development Issues

Raw Materials Acquisition and Processing

- Conservation of natural resources like water, land, and air
- Protection of natural habitats and endangered species
- Waste minimization and pollution prevention, especially the use and release of toxins
- Transportation
- Use of renewable resources; sustainable use of resources
- Use of recycled materials
- Energy consumption

Manufacturing and Distribution Issues

- Minimal use of materials
- Toxic use/release
- By-product/waste generation and handling
- Energy consumption
- Water use
- Emissions to air, land, and water

Product Use and Packaging Issues

- Energy efficiency
- Conservation of natural resources such as water required for the use of the product
- Consumer health and environmental safety

After-Use/Disposal Issues

- Recyclability; ease of reuse, remanufacture, and repair
- Durability
- Biodegradability/compostability
- Safety when incinerated or landfilled

Source: Martin Wolf, Giessen Wolf

An LCI, the first step in conducting a full life cycle analysis of a product, is a process that quantifies the use of energy, resources, and emissions to the environment associated with a product throughout its life cycle. It accounts for the environmental impact of raw-material procurement, manufacturing and production, packaging, distribution, and in-use characteristics straight through to after-use and disposal.

An LCI of cotton versus disposable diapers, for example, would quantify the amount of pesticides and water used to grow cotton, as well as the water and energy needed to manufacture the diapers and transport them to stores and homes. Finally, it would consider the amount of water and energy used to launder the cloth diapers. An LCI of disposable diapers would take into account the environmental implications of cutting down and processing trees for wood pulp, along with the environmental burdens of extraction and refining the petroleum required to produce the plastic backsheets. It would quantify the energy used in manufacturing and transportation, as well as the amount of solid waste eventually sent to landfills. Exhibit 4.2 highlights the results of an LCI commissioned by Procter & Gamble, comparing the relative environmental impacts of cloth versus paper disposable diapers.

Initially developed during the 1970s to help reduce the amount of energy used for developing and distributing products, an LCI is extremely useful for

- comparing the costs associated with energy and resource usage and environmental emissions associated with existing products and their alternatives

- identifying significant areas for reducing energy use and waste

- comparing energy and resource usage and environmental emissions associated with possible alternative ways to manufacture or package products

Exhibit 4.2
Environmental Burdens:
Cloth Versus Disposable Diapers

	Cloth	Disposable
Raw material consumption (lbs.)	3.6	25.3
Water consumption (gal.)	144	23.6
Energy consumption (BTUS)	78,890	23,290
Air emissions (lbs.)	0.860	0.093
Water pollution (lbs.)	0.117	0.012
Solid waste (lbs.)	0.24	22.18

Source: Arthur D. Little, Inc., Disposable versus Reusable Diapers: Health, Environmental, and Economic Comparisons. Report to Procter & Gamble, March 16, 1990

In the past 25 years, several organizations, including Franklin Associates (Prairie Village, Kansas), the Battelle Institute (Columbus, Ohio), Ecobalance (Rockville, Maryland), and the Tellus Institute (Boston, Massachusetts) have performed life cycle inventories in a wide range of industries including paper, paperboard, glass, steel, aluminum, plastic beverage containers and delivery systems, building materials, and transportation products.

Be careful about using life cycle inventory as a marketing tool! Life cycle inventories leveraged for marketing purposes have been criticized for favoring the sponsor. For example, the LCI sponsored by Procter & Gamble comparing cloth versus disposable diapers concluded that when energy and water associated with collecting and washing the cloth diapers were accounted for, the total environmental impact of the cloth diapers was roughly equal to the disposables. This research conflicted with findings from an LCI commissioned by the National Association of Cloth Diaper Services which found cloth to be environmentally superior to disposables. Experts in industry, government, and academia are now working to legitimize the use of the life cycle inventory and other cradle-to-grave approaches as marketing tools. However, given the current state of life cycle analysis and consumer understanding of environment-related product issues, this is likely to be far off in the future.

Proponents of LCI collect all easily available data about a product's life cycle, then prioritize and focus resources on fixing the problems that become apparent early in the analysis process. While improvements are being made, they collect additional data for later incorporation.

As presently developed, life cycle inventory focuses on the raw-material requirements, by-products, waste, and emissions associated with producing a product. However, as demonstrated by the diaper example, it cannot easily differentiate between alternative technologies for addressing the same consumer need. In addition, many environmental concerns are not addressed by LCI. According to Martin Wolf, a consultant on life cycle inventory and green product development, LCI must be augmented with a holistic evaluation of a product's total environmental impact. Renewable or sustainable resource use, habitat destruction, biodiversity depletion, odors, visual pollution, noise pollution, toxicity, biodegradability, and other issues are of concern to environmentalists and consumers but cannot be evaluated by the quantitative approach of LCI and must be considered separately.

STRATEGIES FOR SUCCESS

Many marketers now grow their businesses by addressing the specific environmental issues most relevant to their consumers. In the process, they save money and enhance corporate and brand imagery while ensuring future sales for their products. Use the following strategies to create profitable new or improved products and packages that balance consumers' needs with environmental considerations.

Minimize Direct Environmental Impact

Earth's Best Baby Food

The use of pesticides and fertilizers in crops potentially pollutes soil, water, and atmosphere and also poses a potential threat to the health of humans and wildlife. According to the EPA, about 70 pesticides registered and currently in use are "probable" or "possible" cancer-causers.[2] Children, in particular, are highly vulnerable. On a body-weight basis, children may consume six times as much fruit as adults, and their developing bodies are unable to filter out many of the toxic chemicals.[3]

One company that is attempting to minimize threats posed by unsustainable and unhealthy agricultural practices is Earth's Best, a company recently acquired by the Pittsburgh, Pennsylvania–based H. J. Heinz Company. Earth's Best organic baby food is grown without synthetic pesticides, fertilizers, antibiotics, or growth hormones. It delivers flavorful taste without any preservatives, salt, refined sugar, or modified starches. Reinforcing the concept of a more sustainable product, the glass-jar packaging, made from 30–40 percent recycled content, is recyclable.

Viewed by new parents as an investment in their children's health and future, Earth's Best generated $30 million in sales in 1995, and sales are increasing approximately 20 percent every year.[4] In addition, in some parts of the country, the brand has garnered over 15 percent of the market for strained baby foods despite stiff competition from Gerber, Beechnut, and Heinz. Current sales may represent the tip of the iceberg. With the Earth's Best trademark representing a "seal of approval" for the organic category, H. J.

Heinz may expand the line to adult foods such as soups and sauces, and offer accessories such as pacifiers and baby bottles under the name.[5]

Collins Pine

You don't have to live anywhere near a clear-cut hillside to witness the environmental devastation wreaked by the members of the forest-products industry. Conventional timber practices destroy wildlife habitat, induce soil erosion, increase water pollution, and create ugly scars. The alternative, monoculture tree farms, are vulnerable to insect damage and disease, and they require herbicides and pesticides in order to protect them. Collins Pine of Portland, Oregon, has an even better idea. The company practices sustainable forestry management.

Their forests in California, Pennsylvania, and Oregon represent complex ecosystems of multiple species—ancient trees, bald eagles, and black bears—all managed with the goal of producing high-quality lumber and providing local jobs for generations to come. Each section of the forest is cut on a ten-year cycle, and no more timber is harvested than was produced in the previous decade. Healthy, mature trees are left to grow while aged or diseased trees are felled. Species mix, tree spacing, animal habitat, and other factors are taken into account in deciding which trees to cut. In five decades, Collins Pine has produced 1.5 billion board feet of lumber, yet their forests still contain as much wood as when timber harvesting began.

This highly eco-sensitive practice has helped the company reap estimated sales of more than $100 million per year. Customers include Lexington Furniture Industries, which uses Collins Pine for its Keep America Beautiful line of furniture. For its efforts, the company received the 1996 President's Commission for Sustainable Development Award, one of the newest and most illustrious kudos in the field of green business.[6]

Use Sustainable Sources of Raw Material

The prospect of rapidly depleting stocks of natural resources and the resulting reality of price increases create opportunities for alternative technologies and new efficiency with product design. For example, paper doesn't have to come from trees; in fact, alternative sources may be preferable. Promising new sources include kenaf, a fast-growing bamboo from the southern United States, and hemp, which is naturally pest resistant, can be bleached with peroxide instead of chlorine, and produces a fiber more versatile than fiber from trees.

In 1995, the Tree-Free Ecopaper Company of Portland, Oregon, began producing hemp-based paper made from imported sources (hemp has been outlawed for cultivation in the United States since 1937). The company has sold 700 tons of paper to date and has imported Chinese paper made from hemp and cereal straw. The ban on hemp has kept prices artificially high. The market for Tree-Free's products is expected to grow as the price gap between recycled wood pulp and hemp-based paper narrows.[7]

Natural Fibers Corporation's Ogallala Down

Farming communities from Nebraska through Texas face severe water shortages because the Ogallala Aquifer, a vast reservoir that supplies much of their water, is being rapidly depleted. To cut back on water consumption, some farmers in the region have stopped growing corn, a water-intensive crop.

Herb Knudsen, president of Natural Fibers Corporation, has convinced some of those farmers to grow milkweed—once viewed as an agricultural nuisance—instead. Milkweed is a deep-rooted perennial that conserves water and other natural resources and reduces soil erosion. It also reduces both fertilizer and irrigation requirements compared to raising corn.

Knudsen combines natural downy clusters from milkweed with conventional goosedown to create his Hypodown pillows and comforters. The combination of fibers makes the resulting product hypoallergenic because the milkweed tends to absorb the dust thrown off by the goosedown. The milkweed also makes the product more breathable than goosedown alone. The cost is comparable to similar quality goosedown comforters and pillows.

Hypodown is sold at environmental specialty shops, bedding stores, and major department stores. Since the first Hypodown comforters were manufactured in 1989, more than 30,000 have been sold. Sales doubled in 1995 and are expected to continue a steep incline well into the future. Reports Knudsen, "*Syriaca* (milkweed) is one of the most unused plants in the United States, and every part of the *Syriaca* plant is usable."[8]

Strawbale Construction

Out on Bale, a resource center in Tucson, Arizona, is hard at work engineering a revival of sustainable construction technology with a long history—straw bales. Originally used by Great Plains homesteaders who were confronted by a dearth of trees, straw bales are made of the dead and dried stems of such harvested cereal grains as rice, wheat, oats, and rye. The straw is tightly compressed into rectangular blocks and bound with baling wire, twine, or synthetic cord. Stacked and pinned like bricks on top of a foundation to create exterior building walls, the bales can differ in size, weight, and shape. Interior and exterior finishes can be stucco, plaster, or other materials—even traditional wood siding.

The environmental benefits of strawbale construction are considerable. A strawbale wall has an amazingly high R value of around 50, compared to R 19, the energy efficiency standard for most residential buildings, and its use helps to avoid the 61,000 tons of carbon dioxide that is released each year when millions of tons of straw are otherwise burned. The potential of straw bale is immense. If all the straw in the United States after the harvest of major grains was baled instead of burned, five million 2,000-square-foot homes could be built each year.

Thanks in part to the workshops, technical consultations, and wall-raisings facilitated by Out on Bale since its founding in 1989, hundreds of sustainable structures now exist in diverse climates and locations throughout the United States and other countries. Included among these are the Real Goods Trading Store in Hopland, California, and the Save the Children Headquarters office in Ciudad, Obregon, Mexico.[9]

SOURCE-REDUCE PRODUCTS AND PACKAGING

In the Pollution Prevention Act of 1990, the United States Congress declared "that pollution should be prevented or reduced at its source whenever feasible." Since the cost savings associated with source reduction are roughly parallel to the amount of packaging eliminated,[10] the tenets of this law are not only good for the environment, they are good for business. Less packaging also means less energy required for manufacturing and transportation and less pollution from the production of packaging itself.

To source-reduce, consider lightweighting products and packages. For example, S. C. Johnson's steel aerosol cans use 35 percent less tin than the cans of the late 1980s.[11]

Concentrate products. Superconcentrated laundry detergents, including Lever Brothers' Wisk Power Scoop, now account for half of the $2.1-billion powder laundry cleaners sold in America.[12]

Package in bulk for refilling. Refills used by all-purpose cleaners use less packaging per product and save consumers money. Multipurpose products such as shampoo-and-conditioner-in-one also help to cut down on duplication.

CONSERVE NATURAL RESOURCES, HABITATS, AND ENDANGERED SPECIES

Frigidaire Gallery Tumble-Action Washer

In the United States, groundwater—the primary source of water—is being pumped out faster than it is being replenished. Frigidaire has an idea that can help slow the flow. Using a technology prevalent in Europe, the Frigidaire company has created the Gallery Tumble-Action horizontal-axis washer, which saves 19 gallons of water per load, or more than 8,000 gallons annually, compared to conventional top-loading, vertical-axis washers. This is significant because a life cycle assessment of the environmental impacts of washing machines shows that the vast majority of the environmental impacts occur during the use stage of machine life, *e.g.*, energy and water use (see Exhibit 4.3). Less water to heat converts into energy savings, too—to the tune of over $86 per year.

Here's how it works. Rather than immersing clothes in water, the horizontal-axis washer automatically adjusts the water fill to fit the different load sizes. Instead of using a mechanical agitator, it uses tumble action to simulate hand washing by lifting and plunging clothes through the water over 50 times per minute. Without the mechanical agitator, there is more room for large items.

The Gallery Tumble-Action washer meets the anticipated energy standards for 1999 proposed by the 1992 Energy Policy Act. It is also the first full-size washer to fulfill the efficiency requirements of the Consortium for Energy Efficiency's (CEE) Efficient Clothes Washer Incentive Program. CEE is a nonprofit organization of public utilities and agencies formed to promote energy-efficient technology.

The product, which was launched nationally in October 1996, has done extremely well in test markets, especially in areas with drought and high utility bills.[13]

Teledyne Water Pik's Original Shower Massage Showerhead

The 1992 Energy Policy Act requires all retailers to sell showerheads that deliver a maximum of 2.5 gallons of water per minute. Teledyne has turned this water-conservation mandate into a business. They have designed a complete line of water-saving products that meet this regulation with ease, marketed under the Original Shower Massage brand name.

Exhibit 4.3

Cradle-to-Grave Assessment of Environmental Impacts of Washing Machines

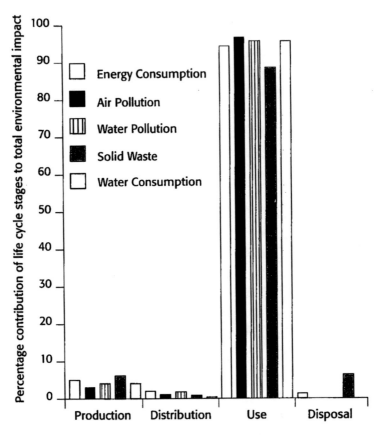

A life cycle assessment of the environmental impacts of washing machines shows that the vast majority of the impacts occur during the use stage of machine life.

Source: "Design for Environment in Practice-Development of the Hoover 'New Wave' Washing Machine." Dr. Robin Roy. The Journal of Sustainable Product Design, *April 1997, p. 39, after PA Consulting Group, 1991. Chart reprinted with permission*

Using a proprietary technology, Teledyne's lineup delivers the performance of a 7-gallon-per-minute shower at the new low 2.5-gallon-per-minute rate. An additional pause setting conserves water during soaping up or shaving by decreasing the flow with a click of the control ring. Packaging is recycled and the product line has received the Green Seal, signifying its environmental merit (see Chapter 7).

This innovation helps to solidify Teledyne's command of the market where the company has been a leader for the past two decades and boasts a 55–58 percent market share.[14] As would be expected, sales of the low-flow products are particularly buoyant in drought areas such as southern California.[15]

International Paper's Triton Paperboard Carriers

Improperly discarded plastic beverage rings kill thousands of waterfowl and other wildlife through entrapment or ingestion. Seizing an opportunity to quell consumer concerns over the unnecessary destruction of wildlife, International Paper now markets Triton brand biodegradable paperboard six-pack carriers.

Made of wood scraps from lumber used for home building and furniture materials, they outperform plastic rings in shake tests and drop tests,[16] and the product is pliable enough to allow animals to break free if caught. If necessary, it can also be recycled with corrugated material. The innovation has attracted more than 25 customers in the bottled-water and fruit juice industries including Smucker Quality Beverages, R. W. Knudsen Family, Santa Cruz Natural, Cascade Clear, and Clearly Canadian.[17]

USE RECYCLED CONTENT

According to the Environmental Defense Fund, recycling

- cuts pollution and conserves natural resources
- conserves energy

- can be cost-competitive with landfilling and incineration if sensibly designed and implemented

- creates jobs and reduces costs in manufacturing sectors that are an important part of our economy.[18]

Recycling also melts away the guilt associated with the 4.3 pounds of garbage each American throws out every day.[19] With the help of innovative technologies, the use of recycled content in consumer products has skyrocketed in the last decade. Products that formerly boasted 10 percent recycled content may now incorporate as much as 100 percent post-consumer content. While even as recently as five years ago, recycled content was limited mostly to paper, glass, metals, and some plastic laundry bottles, now an entire array of high-quality products including clothing, garden furniture, paint, and motor oil are closing the loop.

Wellman, Inc., EcoSpun Fiber

In 1994, Wellman, Inc., of Shrewsbury, New Jersey, the world's largest recycler of PET soda bottles, gave birth to its first branded product, Fortrel EcoSpun™ fiber, made from 100 percent recycled soda bottles. The fiber is sold to mills who turn it into high-quality fabrics.

Depending upon the end-use product, it takes an average of 25 plastic soda bottles to make one garment, and independent testing shows that compared to virgin polyester, the production of EcoSpun uses 60 percent less plastic, emits less carbon dioxide and less sulfur dioxide, and creates fewer hazardous air pollutants than the production of virgin polyester.[20] According to the company, the energy saved by recycling bottles instead of using virgin raw materials can power a city the size of Atlanta for one year.

Not surprisingly, garments made from EcoSpun fibers appeal to outdoor enthusiasts, children, and consumers who believe that protecting the environment is everyone's responsibility. More than

100 manufacturers now opt for EcoSpun over virgin polyester and/or other materials, translating into an exciting new business for Wellman.[21] Patagonia, Levi Strauss, and Eastern Mountain Sports incorporate EcoSpun into their outdoor wear, sleeping bags, sweaters, coats, sportswear, and children's toys.

Scotch Brite Never Rust Wool Soap Pads

3M seized an opportunity to use recycled content in an innovative fashion after focus groups suggested that consumers would love a steel-wool pad that wouldn't rust. The company invented Scotch Brite Never Scratch and Never Rust Wool Soap Pads, made of 100 percent recycled PET plastic impregnated with a phosphorus-free, biodegradable detergent. Using recycled material not only prevents soda bottles from going to landfills and saves energy, it also prevents steel shavings from going down kitchen drains, keeps raw-material costs low, and helps extend product life. Packaging is made from 100 percent recycled paperboard, including 66 percent post-consumer paper. 3M's innovative mix of consumer and environmental benefits has helped Scotch Brite to achieve a 20 percent market share and sales continue to be "very good."[22]

America's Choice Recycled Motor Oil

Each year an estimated 500 million gallons of used lubricating oil seep through landfills and sewers, contaminating local waterways with toxins such as benzene and toluene.[23] Legislation that controls the disposal of used oil is increasing.

Safety Kleen has turned this problem into a business opportunity. Tapping into a network of more than 125,000 service stations, car dealerships, and industrial centers across North America, they collect used motor oil and recycle it into a high-performance, competitively priced product called America's Choice. Their innovative re-refining process converts the components of 100 million gallons of used oil into new lube oil and other usable products.

Volatile solvents become fuel for their manufacturing plant. Heavy distillation residue becomes an asphalt component. Water is treated and discharged as clean water.

With distribution in mass merchandise stores like K-mart and Wal-Mart, Safety Kleen is now the number-one supplier of re-refined oil in the United States, producing 100 million gallons per year in plants in Chicago and Canada.[24]

Crane's "Old Money" and "Denim Blues" Recycled Papers

Crane and Company of Dalton, Massachusetts, makers of high-quality, high-rag-content stationery, now recycle worn currency into a line of "Old Money" stationery. It captures the imaginations of designers, printers, and commercial paper distributors. Big customers include the United States Department of the Treasury; the Institute for Ecolonomics, a nonprofit organization founded by actor and environmental advocate Dennis Weaver; and at least one Federal Reserve branch which uses "Old Money" for its newsletters, annual reports, and letterhead.

Partnered with Levi Strauss and Company, Crane also produces cotton-rag paper made entirely from denim scraps and marketed as "Denim Blues." Representing a new twist in paper recycling, these two "tree-free" initiatives prevent millions of pounds of spent currency and denim scraps from entering landfills, while reducing use of virgin paper products.

MAKE PRODUCTS ENERGY EFFICIENT

Individuals directly consume about 40 percent of the energy used in the United States for such things as powering cars, lighting, heating and cooling homes, and running appliances. In the process, they contribute about 40,000 pounds of carbon dioxide emissions a year. However, many thousands of pounds can be eliminated by simple actions. In fact, the California Energy Commission estimates that cost-effective investments could reduce total U.S. electricity demand by 40 to 75 percent.[25]

Philips Earth Light Compact Fluorescent Lightbulbs

Approximately 25 percent of electricity generated in the United States is used for lighting, costing Americans $32 billion annually[26] and representing the power of more than 100 large 1,000 megawatt plants. Thus, every 1 percent improvement in lighting efficiency can offset the need for a new power plant.

One easy way to save energy is to simply turn off the lights. Another is to switch to energy-efficient bulbs. Philips Lighting now markets a line of compact fluorescent bulbs called the Earth Light Collection. Versatile and attractive, these bulbs save energy and prevent carbon dioxide and sulfur dioxide from being released into the atmosphere.

Although they cost significantly more than incandescents ($15 versus 75¢), their huge energy savings more than offsets the cost of the bulbs over their long lifetime. One Earth Light bulb in a table lamp can save consumers $31 or more in energy costs over its lifetime as compared to a 60-watt incandescent bulb.[27] Because of reduced heat generated by the bulb, it also lowers cooling costs.

While growing slowly in the consumer market considering their high up-front costs, sales are on the rise thanks to educational efforts by Philips and retailers. Grocery stores and supercenters such as Wal-Mart are starting to carry them, too.[28]

EPRI's Microwave Dryer

Conventional dryers use heat from hot air (up to 350°F) to vaporize water in wet clothing. Drying takes time and energy and is hard on clothing. Also, a great amount of waste heat is generated in the process.

The Electric Power Research Institute (EPRI) of Palo Alto, California, has a better idea. They have developed a microwave dryer that dries clothing with a combination of microwave energy and conventional hot air. Moisture is removed quickly and gently at cooler temperatures. A residential model machine dries clothes six times faster than conventional dryers, while a commercial model works in two-thirds the time. Both are about 15 percent more energy efficient.[29]

Because of shorter drying times and more efficient energy use, the microwave dryer helps reduce utility bills. Also, because it is gentler on fabrics, it helps extend the life of clothing. Lower drying temperatures also make the machines suitable for fabrics that would otherwise require dry cleaning, and metal does not pose a problem. Commercial availability is likely in 5 to 7 years at a projected cost of $900–$1,000 versus conventional dryers.[30]

EV-1 Electric Cars from General Motors

Representing just 5 percent of the global population, Americans own one-third of the world's cars and drive about as many miles as the rest of the world combined.[31] As a way to combat air pollution, the California Air Resources Board requires a gradual increase in zero-emission vehicles to 10 percent of all cars marketed by 2003. Because they require only 60–70 percent of the energy consumed by gasoline cars, electric cars and electric gasoline hybrids could greatly improve overall fuel economy.[32]

GM's Saturn Division has announced that it will begin selling an electric two-seater car in four Western markets: Los Angeles, San Diego, Phoenix, and Tucson. EV-1 is a production version of the Impact electric car that GM first showed to the public in 1990. EV-1 will have a driving range of 70–90 miles and will sell in the mid-$30,000 range.

Highly skeptical at first, GM is now a believer. "We didn't think there were enough buyers out there to satisfy the mandate, but we do believe there's an emerging market for these vehicles," admits Frank Schweibold, director of finance and strategy for GM Electric Vehicles in Troy, Michigan.[33]

MAXIMIZE CONSUMER AND ENVIRONMENTAL SAFETY

Scientific data and empirical evidence continue to link various illnesses with consumer products made from synthetic chemicals. According to the EPA, formaldehyde in wood paneling causes wheezing, organic gases in carpeting cause liver damage, perchloroethylene used to dry-clean clothing causes headaches, and VOCs (volatile organic compounds) in cleaning products cause nausea. Many illnesses can be traced to indoor pollution, which has proven to be ten times more toxic than its outdoor counterpart.[34]

Consumers' concerns about product safety translate into opportunities for alternative home construction and cleaning products.

AFM Safecoat and Safechoice Paints

Not too long ago, consumers looking for environmentally safe paints and cleaners had to turn to European products. But consumer demand has spurred domestic manufacturers to offer alternatives of their own.

Nestor Noe, founder of AFM in San Diego, California, began investigating toxic-free building and maintenance products in 1980 when he and his employees were getting sick from conventional products. Today, AFM markets Safecoat and Safechoice brand products, a full line of nontoxic coatings, stains, paints, adhesives, and cleaners made with a water base, as opposed to a chemical base, to industrial and retail consumers. They have found a receptive niche among consumers with chemically related sensitivities, and among such conscientious companies as The Gap, Banana Republic, and Herman Miller looking to safeguard their employees.

Ecomat Wet Cleaning Process

Dry-cleaned clothing harbors a nasty residue — perchloroethylene (perc), a chlorinated hydrocarbon, originally used as an aircraft-degreasing agent in World War II. In significant doses, perc can cause nervous system disorders; headaches; and eye, nose, and throat irritation.[35] It is particularly noxious to workers and individuals living or working in buildings that house dry-cleaning establishments.

Ecomat, a combination cleaners, laundromat, and wash-and-fold franchise founded in 1993, has a better solution. They have achieved a 100 percent reduction of hazardous-waste emissions compared to traditional dry cleaning by adopting their own brand of "multiprocess wet cleaning." It involves a combination of water, natural soaps and oils, steam, and labor skilled at targeting tough spots and stains.

The EPA reports that wet cleaning is economically competitive, performs as well as or better than traditional dry cleaning, and customers like coming to the pleasant facilities.

Now a multimillion-dollar operation cleaning thousands of garments weekly, Ecomat is rapidly developing the New York–New Jersey area as a platform for further growth. As of late 1996, eight stores were in operation, and twenty other franchises have been agreed upon, but not yet opened. Opportunities were also being explored in Malaysia, Thailand, and Australia.[36] With legislation in New York, California, and Massachusetts being proposed to limit use of perc, and considering that wet cleaning represents an economically viable alternative to dry cleaning, Ecomat can look forward to a bright future.

MAKE PRODUCTS MORE DURABLE

As demonstrated by historical sales pitches for Maytag washers and Volvo cars, consumers value durable appliances and automobiles.

Thanks to environmental concerns, long product life will increasingly become a source of added value and an indicator of quality and convenience in many other industries as well.

Lexus Leased Automobiles

Lexus now gives cars a second life as "certified pre-owned cars." Their luxury cars cycle back from rental-car companies or leasors, and wind up in new driveways. "Our problem was somehow to break down the mythology that a used car was someone else's garbage," says Gary Marcotte, manager of special markets for Lexus, a division of Toyota Motor Sales, in Torrance, California. The high quality and durability of Lexus cars impresses customers who would ordinarily desire a brand-new model. Customer testimonials refer to how difficult it is for friends, relatives, and even strangers to tell a used Lexus from a new one. Best yet, selling the pre-owned cars opens a new market for Lexus, which usually targets households earning $200,000 or more annually. Priced at $10,000–14,000 less than a brand-new model, pre-owned Lexus cars are attractive to more middle-class customers.[37]

MAKE PRODUCTS AND PACKAGING REUSABLE OR REFILLABLE

The throwaway convenience culture is making way for reuse and refilling as alternatives to landfilling, incineration, and even recycling.

Rayovac's Renewal Reusable Alkaline Batteries

To power the estimated 900 million toys, phones, smoke detectors, watches, and other battery-operated gadgets now in use, Americans drain 2.5 billion batteries per year. These heavy-metal laced receptacles end up in landfills, with the potential to contaminate groundwater. Traditional rechargeable batteries are not an acceptable environmental alternative. When disposed of, they are the leading source of cadmium in the waste stream, and because cadmium has been linked to kidney and respiratory cancer, many states outlaw their disposal in landfills.

Rayovac offers the battery-consuming public a solution—Renewal, a reusable alkaline battery. Powered with zinc and magnesium, which the FDA categorizes as "Generally Recognized as Safe," Renewal batteries last longer per charge than nicad batteries and, with the help of a special device, can be recharged 25 times or more. Like all alkaline batteries, they are safe for landfill disposal.

At its introduction, Renewal ignited a 31 percent growth in the rechargeable battery industry. It has leapfrogged Millennium and GE/Sanyo to become the number-one rechargeable battery with an impressive segment share of 63 percent. Duracell and Eveready, Rayovac's competitors in the conventional alkaline battery segment, have yet to market a response.[38]

Schroeder's Refillable Milk Bottles

Since the early 1980s, Schroeder of St. Paul, Minnesota, has sold their milk in refillable high-density polyethylene (HDPE) containers to SuperAmerica, a gas/convenience store chain in the Midwest. Customers return empty containers to the stores, which in turn return them to Schroeder's for refilling. Schroeder now adds further value to this process by selling its milk products in returnable and refillable bottles made of LEXAN, a branded polycarbonate resin from GE Plastics.

LEXAN replaces the opaque HDPE with ease. Lighter in weight and with the clarity of glass, it gives milk and other products, such as orange juice, better protection. The containers can be refilled as many as 30–40 times. When the containers can no longer be used, they are recycled into lawn furniture and other products.

Customers love the new packaging and they also like the price. Schroeder's half-gallon-size milk, packaged in LEXAN, sells for several cents less than its refillable HDPE (as well as disposable paperboard) counterparts. Despite flat milk consumption in the upper

Midwest, the company's sales have tripled in the last ten years.[39] Revenues in 1994 were $60 million.

DESIGN PRODUCTS FOR REMANUFACTURING, RECYCLING, AND REPAIR

Landfill disposal bans are in force across the nation for such highly toxic items as lead-acid batteries, tires, used motor oil, paints, and refrigerators. Due to such legislative pressures as well as extended producer responsibility laws in Europe, a growing number of manufacturers now design their products for remanufacture, recycling, and repair, and help set up the infrastructure for doing so. Smart marketers are turning these imperatives into opportunities to save money, enhance quality, and get closer to their customers.

Eastman Kodak's Recyclable Cameras

Eastman Kodak Company solved the problem of forgetting one's camera when they introduced the Kodak Fun Saver 35 one-time-use camera. They later solved the disposal problem by initiating a camera take-back program. Fun Saver cameras are designed so that consumers will not discard them; instead they return the entire camera to a photofinisher for developing. After removing the film for processing, photofinishers are encouraged to return the cameras to Kodak for recycling and reuse. The company reimburses photofinishers for each camera returned and pays the shipping costs.

In late 1996, the company reported that more than 80 million one-time-use cameras had been recycled and/or reused, representing a 77 percent recycling rate. This rate makes one-time-use camera recycling more successful than even aluminum beverage cans, which had a recycling rate of 65.4 percent in 1994.

In all, Kodak says it has diverted more than 10 million pounds of waste from landfills by recycling one-time-use cameras—the equivalent of about 800 tractor loads.[40]

For Kodak, the camera recycling program has generated substantial savings in raw materials and energy since 86 percent of each camera (by weight) is reused; only the lens, battery, and packaging are new, everything else is reused.

MAKE PRODUCTS SAFE FOR DISPOSAL

Amway's SA8 Laundry Concentrate

Consumers think cleaning products should be biodegradable. This implies that ingredients break down quickly and harmlessly after they go down the drain. But not all ingredients are expected to biodegrade. One of these is phosphates, a common ingredient in detergents. They are nutrients readily taken up by water plants. However, when too many of them get into rivers and lakes, they cause algae blooms, robbing the water of oxygen, blocking sunlight, and ultimately killing fish and other marine life. Chlorine is another problem. Although it breaks down, it can react in a harmful way with organic compounds.

Many U.S. detergent manufacturers use zeolites in place of phosphates, but zeolites' environmental superiority to phosphates is under debate. According to *European Chemical News*, the Swedish Water Association found that zeolites produce excessive suspended solids—a source of water pollution—and high oxygen consumption, which can choke plant life when introduced to lakes and streams. Also, detergents with zeolites can fill sewage-treatment systems with up to 40 percent of their weight in solid waste.

Amway Corporation of Ada, Michigan, has created a detergent that makes it a little easier to sift through these issues. Amway's Laundry Care System, SA8® Laundry Concentrate with Bioquest™ Cleaning System, uses naturally derived water softeners instead of phosphates or zeolites to do the cleaning. According to the company, this water softener plus biological enzymes removes stains such as chocolate, blood, grass, and eggs up to three times better than previous Amway non-phosphate laundry concentrates, and biodegradable surfactants do not foam in waterways. Instead, they break down into carbon dioxide and water and other harmless, naturally occurring compounds. Also, the natural water softeners it contains break down in the environment to water and naturally occurring minerals.

Given that 50 percent of the United States population is currently under some kind of phosphate regulatory restriction and zeolites are under question, this product looks like it may just be a winner for Amway as well as the environment. Introduced in January 1996, the company reports that initial sales are substantially exceeding expectations.[41]

MAKE PRODUCTS AND PACKAGING COMPOSTABLE

In nature, everything is recycled. Waste for one organism becomes food for another. According to the EPA, approximately 40 percent of our solid wastes are biodegradable materials that can be effectively composted into humus, an organic matter that can enrich gardens and agricultural soils. This has important implications for businesses, and a number of innovative designers are developing products with this idea in mind.

EcoPLA Renewable Biopolymers from Cargill

Americans consume 60 billion pounds of plastics per year, but because plastics don't biodegrade and are not widely recycled, an estimated 6 billion pounds wind up in landfills.[42]

Plastic improperly disposed of on land or in water can seriously impact marine life and waterfowl, and, by one estimate, plastics, along with discarded fishing gear, kill one million seabirds annually—in 128 species around the world.[43] According to the Center for Marine Conservation, 58 percent of the three million pounds of debris collected in 1994 during an annual cleanup of U.S. waterways was plastic.

Now, fully biodegradable polymers made primarily from agricultural products such as corn hold promise for creating new recycling/recovery options for plastic packaging, food service, and home products. ECOPLA (*Eco* for ecology, *PLA* for polylactide) made by Cargill of Minneapolis, Minnesota, is a promising new biodegradable polymer developed by scientists seeking new uses for corn. ECOPLA, derived from corn seed, is both compostable and recyclable. It can be totally degraded through composting, eventually turning into water, carbon dioxide, and humus just like paper.

Because ECOPLA is both strong and versatile, it can be transformed into sturdy bags for collecting yard trimmings, food scraps, and single-use disposables such as plates, cups, straws, and packaging materials.[44]

IDEAS FOR ACTION

Use the following checklist to explore the myriad opportunities for refining existing products or developing new ones that meet environmental imperatives and satisfy consumers' primary demands.

Raw Material Procurement

- Can we minimize the potential for our raw-materials-procurement process to avoid tropical deforestation? Land stripping? Oil spills?

- Can we use renewable resources or resources that are sustainably managed?

Manufacturing

- What steps can we take to prevent or otherwise reduce the production of solid and hazardous waste in our manufacturing processes? How can we reduce our use of water? Emissions to air and waterways?

Use

- Can we redesign our products to make them more energy- or resource-efficient and thereby reduce operating costs?

- Can we make our products safer or more pleasant to use?

- Can we use alternative ingredients that help to minimize risks to health and the environment?

After-Use Recovery and Disposal

- Can we design our products to be durable? Refillable? Reusable? Repairable? Remanufacturable? Rechargeable?

- Can we redesign our products or packages to reduce the need for landfilling?

- Can we make our products and packaging safer to landfill or incinerate?

- Can we use materials and ingredients that are inherently biodegradable or compostable?

Notes

1. Gillespie, Robert S., "The Environment: Opportunities for Responsible Business," presentation to the Association of National Advertisers, October 28, 1991.
2. Lefferts, Lisa, "A Commonsense Approach to Pesticides," *Nutrition Action Health Letter*, Volume 20, Number 7, p. 5.
3. Reid, Craig, "Don't Get Bugged by Insecticides," *Vegetarian Journal*, January/February 1995, p. 23.
4. Telephone conversation with Lisa Bell, July 9, 1996.
5. Cropper, Carol Marie, "Bringing Up Baby with Its Parents on the Sideline," *New York Times*, May 5, 1996, p. 12.

6. "The Company That Broke the Logjam," *In Business*, July/August 1995, p. 35, and personal communication with Wade Mosby, April 2, 1996.

7. "Paper Without Trees," *Popular Science*, March 1996, p. 32.

8. Natural Fibers Corporation press release, February 1996, p. 1.

9. Telephone conversation with Darren Port, Green Logic Design, May 22, 1997, and Judy Knox, Out on Bale, May 23, 1997.

10. *Green Packaging 2000*, February 1994, p. 4.

11. Johnson, S. C., *Partners Working for a Better World*, February 1992, p. 10.

12. *Household and Personal Products Industry*, January 1992, p. 42.

13. Conversation with Cheri Shepherd, merchandising manager, July 11, 1996.

14. Personal communication with Kurt McKamy, March 9, 1992.

15. Personal communication with Russ Mackay, July 15, 1996.

16. Triton sales literature.

17. Conversation with Rob Heimbach, marketing manager, July 15, 1996.

18. Denison, Richard, and John Ruston, "Recycling Isn't Garbage," Environmental Defense Fund memorandum, July 19, 1996.

19. "Municipal Solid Waste Recovery Rate Surpasses 20%," *Reusable News*, U.S. Environmental Protection Agency, Winter 1995, p. 1.

20. Diesenhouse, Susan, "Polyester Becomes Environmentally Correct," *New York Times*, February 20, 1994, p. B9.

21. *Ibid.*

22. Personal communication with Deborah Johnson, product representative at 3M, June 26, 1996.

23. Brinkman, Dennis, "Used Oil: Resource or Pollutant?"

Technology Review, July 1985, p. 47.

24. Telephone conversation with John Paul Kusz, February 26, 1997.

25. Peterson, John, "Behavior Change," *Road to 2015*, p.156.

26. Walker, Kenneth, *Power Boosters: Ohio's Energy Efficiency Success Stories*, July 1995, p. 37.

27. "Earth Light Collection," Philips press release. Spring 1996, p. 3.

28. Personal communication with Steve Goldmacher, Philips director of public relations, July 24, 1996.

29. Electric Power Research Institute news release, April 1996, p. 1.

30. Telsen, Laurie, "Microwave Dryer Wins Popular Science 'Best of What's New Award,'" *Electric Power Research Institute News*, November 15, 1996.

31. "Energy Efficiency," *Renew America, Sharing Success*, Volume 1, Number 3, 1992, p. 1.

32. Peterson, John, *Road to 2001*, p. 174.

33. Fisher, Lawrence M., "GM, in a First, Will Sell a Car Designed for Electric Power This Fall," *New York Times*, January 5, 1996, p. A10.

34. Sheridan, Frances, "Is Your Home Healthy?" *E Magazine*, May/June 1996, p. 44.

35. *Rachel's Environmental and Health Weekly*, Number 431, March 2, 1995.

36. Personal communication with Keith R. Emerson, vice president, franchise development, Ecomat, February 25, 1997.

37. Ramirez, Anthony, "Lexus Puts a New Spin on the Rundown Image of Used Cars," *New York Times*, August 10, 1995, p. D3.

38. Telephone conversation with John Daggett, Rayovac, July 1996.

39. Davies, Paul, "Shroeder's Legacy," *Twin Cities Business Monthly*, March 1995.

40. Kodak press release, May 8, 1996.

41. Personal communication with Jim Kucera, manager of Home Living, August 8, 1996.

42. "Renewable Bioplastic a Reality," *Green Design*, Winter 1994, p. 5.

43. "Fridges, Fabrics, and Fowl," *E Magazine*, March/April 1996, p. 64.

44. Personal conversation with Steven Mojo, consultant to Cargill, December 10, 1996.

5

The Next Big Product Opportunity

Many green products on the market today represent small enhancements or "tweaks" to existing ones. Recycled content replaces virgin materials; packaging is lighter or designed to be refilled; washing machines save water and energy by tumbling clothes on a horizontal as opposed to a vertical axis. Although these are admirable and much-needed technical achievements, the reductions in environmental impact they represent may not be enough to meet future consumer needs in a sustainable fashion.

Finding solutions to environmental degradation involves much more than replacing one supermarket cartful of goods with another. That is because our present modes of production and consumption are simply not sustainable — "sustainability" is defined as meeting the needs of the present without compromising the ability of future generations to meet their own needs — in the face of a global population that is 5.8 billion today and expected to reach 10 billion by 2040.

Some experts go so far as to estimate that achieving sustainability over the next few decades requires a radical change in the entire production and consumption of industrial societies—a "system discontinuity," characterized by a 90 percent reduction in the consumption of environmental resources.[1] Societies that run at 90 percent "eco-efficiency" eat lower on the food chain (*i.e.*, more plants and legumes as opposed to animal-based proteins); minimize the use of raw materials by recycling, reusing, and other means; and generate energy from renewable as opposed to fossil-fuel sources, which are not only quickly depleting but also contribute to global climate change and acid rain.

The issue of sustainability is especially critical for U.S. consumers. The United States represents 5 percent of the world's population but consumes 30 percent of the world's natural resources and creates 50 percent of global greenhouse gases. Since 1900, the U.S. population has tripled, while procurement of natural resources has multiplied 17 times.[2] Clearly, this is not sustainable. With developing countries looking to adopt Western lifestyles, pressures on global natural resources will intensify. Entire ecosystems such as the Florida Everglades are at risk of collapse.

Great strides are being made in the areas of information technology and "nano-technology," which uses resources superefficiently by building products one atom at a time. However, technological advances may not be enough. Major shifts in lifestyle will be necessary, as well as significant changes in how we meet basic human needs through the products and services we buy. We must leap rather than tweak.

Clearly, caring for the needs of a burgeoning population in a sustainable fashion presents opportunities for innovative companies. The purpose of this chapter is to provide a framework for thinking about solving environmentally related consumer issues creatively, and in doing so, offer some inspiration from history's preeminent problem-solver—Mother Nature.

What Is Green?

Green products are typically durable, nontoxic, made from recycled materials, or minimally packaged. Of course, there are no completely green products, for they all use up energy and resources and create by-products and emissions during their manufacture, transport to warehouses and stores, usage, and eventual disposal. So green is relative, describing those products with less impact on the environment than their alternatives.

Ask the question "What is green?" If any certainty exists at all, too often the answer is "It depends." That's because the factors that make a product "green" often depend upon the specific product or product category, where it will be used, how often, by whom, and for what reason.

What Is the Product Category?

Biodegradability, for example, may be a highly desirable feature for laundry detergents whose suds can pollute local waterways, but it may not be relevant for paper cups or plastic trash bags destined for landfills where decomposition occurs slowly, if at all, and stability—if the landfill is to support a new airport, for instance—is preferred. Conventional alkaline batteries are considered green if they contain no added mercury, but they are highly toxic nevertheless, because of the other materials they contain.

Where Will the Product Be Used?

What might be green in my backyard may not be green in yours, because regional variations may exist in the amount or types of natural resources available, the local climatic and topographical conditions, and whether reduction, reuse, recycling, or composting are options. In a country as diverse as the United States, such conditions can vary dramatically from state to state, even from town to town. So, broadly speaking, washable cloth diapers may be environmentally preferable in the Northeast where landfill space is at a premium and water is plentiful, but may be less desirable in the Southwest where water supplies are tight and there are still plenty of potential spots to bury trash. Because they take up less space, plastic supermarket bags may actually be environmentally preferable to paper bags where landfilling is the only option, but in areas where composting is a possibility, paper might be the optimal eco-choice.

How Will It Be Used?

Is a product likely to be used once and thrown away, or used over and over again? According to one chemist, if a ceramic mug will not be used at least 1,000 times, then the energy it takes to make it doesn't justify its presumed environmental preferability over polystyrene.[3] Compact fluorescent lightbulbs cost more than incandescents for a reason: all those weighty materials consume a lot of energy in their manufacture and transport. If they are used in lamps that are turned on and off frequently, the long-term energy savings likely won't be realized; incandescents may be preferable.

Are Alternative Technologies Available?

Environmental impact is literally designed into products up front. So existing products can only be tweaked so much before a jump to an entirely new or different technology capable of filling the same consumer need is necessary to make a significant improvement in environmental performance. For example, no amount of tinkering with incandescent lightbulbs (which throw off 90 percent of their energy in excess heat) will ever achieve the cooler-burning efficiency of compact fluorescents. Use recycled envelopes and stationery, fill the trucks with natural gas, but E-mail will always be environmentally preferable to even the greenest conceivable "snail mail."

Making "green" even tougher to pin down is the fact that no

agreed-upon method exists to measure the precise relative environmental impact of one product against alternatives. In the debate over cloth versus disposable diapers, for example, value judgments come into play—plastic and paper production and solid waste, or cotton production and the water and energy to wash the diaper?

What Comes Next?

Environmental issues are constantly changing, reflecting new discoveries such as the hole in the ozone layer, shortages in natural resources, population shifts, and fewer places to bury everyone's trash. Technology is constantly advancing. Consumer tastes and attitudes evolve. Laws and marketing strategies are rewritten accordingly. Thus, no matter how well companies do their homework, what is accepted as "green" today may wind up being viewed as "brown" tomorrow. The aerosol industry and McDonald's learned this the hard way.

In the late 1970s, in response to reports linking chlorofluorocarbons to ozone layer depletion and subsequent consumer outcry, the aerosol-packaging industry quickly switched to hydrocarbon-based propellants. However, we now know that hydrocarbons create smog when mixed with sunlight; so the move is on to find a viable alternative, lest further sales be lost to pumps and other competitive technologies.

Since the 1970s, the packaging for McDonald's hamburgers has evolved from one technology to another in response to environmental as well as economic considerations. First, polystyrene foam replaced paper, but then was replaced altogether by quilt wraps. This much-heralded, source-reduced alternative may one day be replaced itself by compostable packaging, now in test. Environmentally speaking, the folks at McDonald's can't rest. Because of escalating global food demands, coupled with the environmental degradation associated with cattle-raising, the very beef in McDonald's Big Macs may soon be under fire regardless of whether it is produced domestically or in the Amazon rain forest.

With green a moving target, planning gets tricky; industry can only respond as quickly as the market demands. This poses the risk of rushing greener products to market to serve the demands of influential consumers while mass consumers may be unaware of the need for a change. The green marketplace is rife with examples of less than perfect timing such as the following:

- When competitors were moving toward ½-cup laundry detergent concentrations, Church & Dwight answered with a ¼-cup formula for their own Arm & Hammer ultraliquid brand. But their sales suffered from confusion over the ½-cup "compacts" of other manufacturers. Acknowledging that consumers were prepared for only so much greenness at a time, the company reneged on the more concentrated alternative.[4]

- Introduced in response to a newly discovered need of chemophobics, Heinz's Cleaning Vinegar, a double-strength version of its normal product, flopped when introduced into supermarkets as an alternative cleaning aid. The mass consumer didn't seem to know what to make of it. While greater consumer marketing and educational efforts no doubt would have helped enhance its chance of success, the product opportunity may have been better served by a niche strategy, distributing the product in health-food stores and green-product catalogs until enough of the mass market was prepared to switch to the ecologically conscious offering.

Lack of precise definitions for "green" coupled with the "moving target" syndrome tend to discourage industry from making the long-term investments needed to develop new technologies and market the greener products that result. Recent history is rife with examples of industry losing its sticking power in the face of market uncertainty for green technologies. Solar power is just one case in point.

After a rush of government funding in response to the oil crisis of the mid-1970s, U.S. industry geared up to develop photovoltaics (solar) technology. But when oil became cheap and plentiful again, and the Reagan Administration withdrew support for the fledgling technologies, industry sold outstanding key patents to Japan, a country deficient in natural-energy sources. The Japanese now hold the lead in this key future energy source. There is hope that American industry has learned that when it comes to the environment, it pays to think ahead.

NEED TO THINK IN NEW WAYS

Environmental concerns force today's consumers to question their assumptions about what types of products best meet their needs. Paper no longer has to be white. Recycled content, once deemed inferior—even unclean—is now preferable to virgin. Disposable products, once associated with feelings of satisfaction (we were so rich as a country we could afford to throw things away!), make us feel guilty.

Question your own assumptions. Reevaluate your business strategies. Think differently about what it takes to meet basic human needs in a sustainable fashion. In the not-too-distant future, advantage will accrue to corporations that can transcend existing paradigms and product categories, redefining existing notions of how best to meet consumer needs. The future belongs to companies that can invent new designs, materials, and technologies that meet consumer needs with minimal, if not zero, environmental impact. It belongs to companies who can reinvent how existing industries operate, or create entirely new industries if necessary.

Address consumers' concerns credibly and profitably by integrating environmental issues into new-product planning and overall corporate strategy, as follows.

Be Pro-Active

Because availabilities of natural resources are in constant flux, new materials and technologies are forever being developed. Learning is always taking place. So, be ever-vigilant and plan ahead.

Address Green Continuously

Because green is a "moving target," unexpected shifts in consumer sensibilities can occur with the potential to wipe out entire markets or tarnish corporate reputations. So address environmental issues on a continuous basis in order to better anticipate such consumer shifts, control your own destiny, and steal a march on competitors when the time to respond approaches.

Address Environmental Issues at the Design Stage

We cannot "tweak" our way to green. Design products and their packages *up front* to balance environmental challenges and consumers needs most satisfactorily. The introduction of the Woody Pen, marketed by the Goodkind Pen Company of Scarborough, Maine, demonstrates this strategy well.

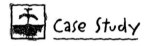 Case Study **Woody Pens: Designed for the Environment**

Rather than making its pens of plastic, Goodkind Pen Company uses birch scraps sourced from local furniture makers, and its pens are designed to be refillable. As an alternate to conventional "blister" packs, Goodkind Pen displays its pens in an innovative plastic clamshell that can be reused and recycled. Consumers simply unsnap the package components, remove the pen and its refill, and drop the package in a mailbox so that it can be returned to Goodkind.

By carefully designing its product up front for minimal environmental impact, Goodkind yields a product with a super-green profile and, in the process, enjoys a high level of satisfaction from both environmentally conscious consumers, as well as other consumers who enjoy the comfort and economic benefits of using a refillable wood-based pen.

Change the System, Not the Product

Environmental issues are holistic in nature. Often the most significant environmental impacts occur when the entire system of design, manufacturing, distribution, and reuse/disposal is overhauled, rather than just one or two features of a specific product or package. Knoll Furniture reduced packaging required for new office installations by 90 percent by lining the trucks and amending the loading docks rather than by "tweaking" the wrappings on individual pieces of furniture.

As a way to cut out milk-carton-type packaging altogether, Coca-Cola has explored siphoning syrup directly from trucks into holding bins at fountains and fast-food restaurants. In California, an entrepreneur sells carbonated-water taps along with syrup so consumers can make popular brands of soft drinks like Diet Coke and Sprite at home. His innovation represents a packaging and energy-saving alternative to pre-mixed bottles of pop that need to be transported to and from stores.

Changing the system by which products are designed and sold—or shall we say, changing the way benefits are delivered or consumer needs are met—suggests many opportunities for resource and energy-saving innovation, such as integrating products within the household infrastructure. Such staples as sugar, flour, salt, and pepper are sold in bulk, ready to be transferred within the home to permanent packages like sugar bowls, salt and pepper shakers, canisters, and the like. Similarly, household paper towels and toilet tissue are designed to fit neatly into permanent wall mounts. Why not consider selling permanent packages for your own products?

Some permanent packages are already finding their way onto supermarket shelves. Church & Dwight, for example, markets a refillable plastic shaker for its Arm & Hammer baking soda. Good Seasons salad dressing mix has long been accompanied by a free glass cruet. Liquid household and personal-care products, such as shampoos, liquid dishwashing detergents, and other cleaners, are starting to be sold in bulk for transferral to dispensers inside the home. Opportunities exist to market attractive dispensers. Given the flimsy nature of some spray bottles, an opportunity exists for manufacturers to sell permanent, dishwasher-safe packages designed for use with the collapsible-pouch packages now marketed as refills for popular household cleaning products.

One company that believes in the potential for permanent packaging is Rubbermaid, makers of Litterless Lunch Kits. Designed to replace brown bags, juice boxes, plastic baggies, and foil wraps, the kits are durable and reusable and come in an array of sizes and styles. For example, a whimsical Gilbert the Fish appeals to kids under five. Gilbert provides easy access to lunch through his oversized mouth, which unzips to fold down as a place-mat. His tail fin hides a zippered compartment for milk money, keys, and other small items. Sold at Wal-Mart and grocery stores, the lunch kits retail from about $10.[5]

Consider refillables at retail. Where allowed by law, The Body Shop allows consumers to refill cosmetics jars from a special refill bar. In Germany, consumers refill milk bottles from a steel cow. The potential for refilling suggests the prospect of in-store "real estate" for product manufacturers. Individual brands of cereal and coffee, for example, would be allotted permanent dispenser space on store shelves.

Be Flexible

Since environmental ills can vary by region as well as from season to season, opportunities exist for new market segmentations and line extensions akin to those used by sophisticated packaged-good marketers. Consider coffee.

Coffee drinkers have it made. At the supermarket shelf, they can pick among all-method grinds, drips as well as instant, freeze-dried, whole bean, and coffee-for-one "tea" bags. Coffee enthusiasts can shun the regular stuff for flavored coffees like French Vanilla and Swiss Mocha Almond, as well as espresso and the exotic blends like Arabian Mocha Sanai sold in specialty shops.

Depending upon the distribution channel and the brand, packages can be steel cans, glass, aseptic packs, or kraft paper bags.

Marketers of green products can adopt similar flavor, formulation, and packaging variations. With the diversity of green issues around the country and around the world, a customized approach may represent the best chance for minimizing environmental impact.

Diversify Offerings

For example, allow consumers to choose packages made of materials that accommodate local capabilities for recycling, composting, or landfilling. Differentiate on the basis of product formulation. Melitta, for example, simultaneously markets both unbleached and bleached white coffee filters.

Although it sounds counterintuitive, offering a product with a "greener" profile right alongside one's historical "brown" product does not necessarily send a conflicting message about a company's green commitment. Empirical evidence suggests consumers are grateful for the choice. From a practical standpoint, the marketing of "greener" products alongside traditional offerings helps to serve the needs of that broad swath of consumers who may not yet be acting upon certain environmental issues, while having an alternative handy when they are ready to "trade up." Some marketers choose to avoid this dilemma in the first place through selective distribution strategies, alternative branding, or discontinuing the conventional product/technology at the "greener" one's introduction.

Take the High Road

Maximize the long-term payout of product development efforts by adopting the most environmentally sound technology, materials, or designs possible within the constraints of economics and consumer acceptance. This can also provide opportunities to preempt competition and avoid costly legislation. In the process, it can pay off in positive publicity and enhanced brand and corporate imagery often associated with leadership.

 Case Study   **The McDonough Collection: Textiles with Zero Impact**

The William McDonough Collection of environmentally preferable fabrics manufactured by DesignTex Inc., of New York City, is just one example of a product line with the lofty goal of zero environmental impact. Created by the designer and architect for which it was named, the collection relies on a proprietary process that eliminates all toxic by-products at every step in the manufacturing process; the factory effluent actually leaves cleaner than it was when it came in! What's more, the fabric actually biodegrades safely into soil, leaving no carcinogens, persistent toxic chemicals, heavy metals, or other harmful substances. (Compare this to the estimated 127 heavy metals in the average silk tie!)

For the fabric, McDonough chose natural wool from New Zealand and ramie from the Philippines that is compostable and grown without pesticides or synthetic fertilizers. The fabrics are then dyed with a selection of only 16 pigments culled from a possible 4,500 commonly used in textiles that could be manufactured without releasing pollutants. By-products from the weaving process are shipped to strawberry farms near the manufacturing plant in Heerervegg, Switzerland, where the biodegradable scrap fabric is used in place of plastic as ground cover.

The fabrics have found a ready market among high-end furniture manufacturers, designers, and architects who appreciate its uncompromising attention to aesthetics as well as its environmental sensibilities.

Rethink the Value Your Products Provide

When it comes right down to it, consumers don't really *need* cellular telephones, designer clothing, or subcompact cars. They need to communicate, to stay warm, and to be transported from place to place. And if you really think about it, consumers don't need to *own* products per se; what they really need is the *utility* such products provide. Take a giant mental leap forward by rethinking your own products with these concepts in mind! You'll likely discover innumerable fresh new opportunities to increase profits and enhance customer loyalty. As long as you're thinking big, go so far as to consider selling *services* as replacements for, or adjuncts to, material products.

As identified by various, mostly European, experts working in what might just wind up to be the most exciting area of new product development in the future, four different groups of services are possible:

- Product-life extension services—services designed to extend the life of products, *e.g.*, technical assistance, repair, maintenance, and disposal service

- Product-use services—the sharing of products as well as using products for some time without the need to buy, *e.g.*, a "Greenwheels" car-sharing service now offered in the Netherlands

- Intangible services—substituting products for labor-based services, *e.g.*, automated bill-paying and in-home voice mail as a replacement for answering machines

- Result services—services designed with the aim of reducing the need for material products, *e.g.*, pedestrian access rather than cars, urban recreation facilities rather than forced tourism[6]

Does your product pose a solid-waste challenge in terms of bulk and/or toxics? Consider leasing rather than selling it outright. Leasing provides an opportunity to maintain control over one's product throughout its entire life cycle. This translates to a cost-effective source of raw materials and it can help reduce liabilities stemming from irresponsible disposal by others. To reap these benefits, some chemical companies now lease their products, and some office equipment manufacturers now lease rather than sell copy machines. Although not marketed as such, manufacturers of toner cartridges who take their products back at the end of their useful lives (in this case, by providing for free pick-up at consumers' homes and offices) are in effect leasing the use of their products.

Many manufacturing companies can easily sell services as an adjunct or as a replacement to their own or another company's products. Appliance makers such as GE and Whirlpool already enjoy hefty revenues from service contracts. Electric-power utilities sell energy-conservation services in addition to power. Manufacturers of electric power mowers would do well to consider selling Xeriscaping services—using water-conserving native shrubs and grasses in water-short areas, for example—or potentially lose out to competitors outside their category. Ridding one's dress shirt of a greasy stain takes knowhow in addition to soap and elbow grease. Prediction: in addition to converting natural resources into Ajax and Biz, the big soap companies will convert *human resources* into paid-telephone-advice lines on spot removal.

Consider services, too, for their potential to lock in customers over time. It can be said that Ametek (see Chapter 8) is in the business of helping Ethan Allen protect furniture rather than manufacturing polypropelene. Instead of selling a product once, consider leasing, or even giving the product away and selling the refills. Think of the opportunities for manufacturers of coffeemakers, electric toothbrushes, and soap dispensers, all of whom have an incentive to make their initial products more durable, too.

Getting Started: Ask "How Would Mother Nature Do It?"

The most fertile source of inspiration for companies in search of innovative methods to meet consumers' needs in environmentally sound ways is Mother Nature herself. For centuries, product and package designers have been inspired by her ingenious designs and technologies. Think about it. Cameras mimic the human eye. Helicopters hover and fly backward like hummingbirds. Velcro fasteners adopt the same entangled architecture as the prickly burrs attached to their Scottish inventor's boot.

By definition, green products are more nature-like: they are inherently efficient, easy to recycle, and often driven by solar power. Consider some of the greener products and technologies on the market today. ENERGY STAR computers save on energy by hibernating when not in use. Solar cells on the roof of Mazda's 929 run a ventilating system when the car is parked in the sun. Like peas in a pod, rolls of Kodak film stacked in one box instead of sold separately cut down on packaging waste.

The principles of nature have been incorporated into a creativity process invented by the author to generate concepts for new products and services that represent minimal environmental impact. Some of the strategies contained in this *Getting to Zero*^{SM} process include the following:

Keep It Simple

A banana peel is a deceptively simple package. It protects its contents, it is easy to open, it eliminates the need for utensils, and it signals when its contents are ripe. How many human-designed packages can claim as much?

Trees are equally elegant in a multipurpose sort of way. When alive, they provide food, shelter, and shade, not to mention inspiration for poetry and a place of lofty refuge for kids. When naturally felled in the forest, they become food and home for a whole new host of organisms and wildlife. When felled by humans, they provide any number of useful products including paper, furniture, and wooden pencils.

In packaging a key to simplicity is source reduction — using designs that require less material in the first place. Since source reduction means the elimination of the very bells and whistles that make some types of packaging so convenient, this can be tricky. Colgate-Palmolive addressed this issue literally quite neatly in designing a new toothpaste tube that eliminated the need for an outer carton.

Colgate-Palmolive proved that one doesn't have to give up convenience in a source-reduced package when they introduced stand-up tubes in the fall of 1992. Prompted by retailers in Germany, where customers have the right to leave unwanted packaging behind, Colgate's innovation eliminates the traditional outer carton by allowing the tube to stand on its own via the use of a flat-top pad nozzle. Because it is powered by gravity, it solves the age-old problem of emptying the tube completely — a worthy environmental goal all by itself.

The revolutionary new tube design uses 20 percent less primary packaging material than a regular laminated tube and it has only four parts compared to as many as ten components in typical pumps. It also costs less than a pump. In the United States, it has attracted a loyal following of consumers who like its heightened convenience: the vertical storage feature keeps the toothpaste ready to dispense, and improves neatness and ease of use.

Grow Your Products Green

Nature's own economy is plant based and solar based. Biologically based products are starting to displace alternatives made from chemicals on supermarket shelves. Liquid Plummer, for example, markets a drain cleaner that uses the power of enzymes to literally eat through food and grease. Some consumers prefer cleaners that are made from d-limonene, nature's own solvent, extracted from orange peels in the orange-juice-making process.

Consider the stories of Fox Fibre and Citra-Solv, two innovative natural products on the market today.

Case Study   Fox Fibre:
Dyed by Nature

Consumers know that a bright, white cotton T-shirt feels natural. What they don't know is that it takes tons of herbicides and pesticides and millions of gallons of water to grow the cotton plants, which are sprayed with a chemical defoliant to prevent leaf-staining. The resulting fiber is then saturated with bleach, or dyed with any number of potentially toxic chemicals.[7]

Sally Fox, founder of Natural Cotton Colours, Inc., of Wickenberg, Arizona, has a better idea: she grows cotton that is colored naturally. Fox discovered that ancient peoples grew their cotton in bright colors. After ten years of experimentation, she produces cotton that yields beautifully colored fibers in hues of brown and green (she is currently working on blue). Her colored cotton is also naturally resistant to pests, so it requires fewer pesticides than conventional cotton. Also, because the resulting fabrics are naturally colorfast, there's no fading. In fact, the colors actually intensify with the first fifteen washings. The hues are naturally warm and elegant.

Starting with a mere six plants, Fox's business now grows enough product to supply cotton to yarn spinners in ten different countries. Companies such as Fieldcrest, IKEA, and Levi Strauss use this company's naturally colored fibers in their products. Timing has contributed to success—people concerned about the environment are drawn to Fox Fibre for its unique characteristics and are also willing to pay a slight premium. In 1993, when L. L. Bean first offered a Fox Fibre sweater for $39, it sold out in a week.[8]

Case Study — Citra-Solv: Nature's Own Cleaner

In a marketplace where all the leading products are made from a profusion of sometimes nasty-sounding synthetic chemicals, Shadow Lake's Citra-Solv® cleaner and degreaser stands apart. It is made almost entirely from d-limonene, nature's own degreaser, extracted from orange peels left over from the juice-making process.

Citra-Solv was originally created for the commercial and industrial markets. When OSHA regulations required that chemicals used in cleaning products be disclosed on product labels, Steven and Melissa Zeitler, founders of Shadow Lake, Inc., got the idea to take the product retail when employees, enamored with the product's fresh orange smell, asked to take some home.

Helping to debunk the myth that "green" products don't work as well as their "brown" counterparts, Citra-Solv quickly rubs out lipstick stains, chewing gum, adhesive goo, and easily tackles greasy barbecue grills and automobile wheel rims.

Distributed in over 90 percent of health-food stores and environmental-product catalogs, where it is typically a bestseller, and now a growing number of specialty-food stores, Citra-Solv represents a multimillion-dollar business. A recent partnership with the USDA's Alternative Agricultural Research and Commercialization Corporation providing marketing support promises to grow this product made from renewable resources even further.

Think in Circles

In nature there's no such thing as waste everything is recycled. Soil, for example, represents decomposed plant and animal matter poised to support new life. Water is constantly being transformed in a neverending cycle consisting of evaporation, condensation, rainfall, and evaporation.

A growing brood of "industrial ecologists" now urges manufacturers to shift their thinking from a linear "cradle-to-grave" mode to a more circular "cradle-to-cradle" approach. Their recommended strategies—recycling, reuse, remanufacturing, and composting—all represent opportunities to create valuable new uses for products that would otherwise be dead-ended in landfills.

As Xerox has discovered, thinking in circles provides opportunities to save money and maximize return on assets through recycling and reuse of materials or components. New markets can be created for goods that are refurbished and resold. By thinking in circles, John Deere saves money and avoids landfill issues through an innovative reusable packaging system.

 **Case Study** **Xerox: Where Thinking in Circles Pays Off**

Xerox Corporation is a big believer in remanufacturing. No wonder. They have saved $200 million in materials and parts cost in less than five years by remanufacturing some of their copiers, using the same assembly line to produce newly manufactured as well as remanufactured machines.

In Europe, Rank Xerox markets the two types of machines as separate product lines. The lower-cost remanufactured line allows Xerox to competitively price against other manufacturers; in the United States, the machines are sold in the same product line. The remanufactured machines match Xerox's high expectations for new machines, and according to company surveys, consumer acceptance of the remanufactured machines, which come with a three-year performance guarantee, has increased in the past five years.[9]

Try recycling the wastes of another industry, or look for innovative ways for other manufacturers to turn your own waste into gold. The toy industry has created a huge market for the integrated circuit boards that are quickly made obsolete by rapid advances in computer chip technology. In a most symbiotic way, the used-chip market has flourished due to the growth in the number of toys utilizing computer technology, while the toy industry benefits from the availability of low-cost chips.[10]

 Case Study   **John Deere Saves
Money Through Reuse**

The John Deere Company of Horicon, Wisconsin, enjoys the opportunity it created to save money by pioneering the notion of reusable shipping crates. It chooses to go beyond compliance of state laws prohibiting the landfilling or burning of corrugated containers and opts for reusable/returnable plastic containers for the 5,000-plus components arriving at its farm-equipment factories. Deere, which owns the containers, provides them to its parts suppliers for shipping tractor components to assembly plants; the assembly plants return the empties in a continuous loop. Made of high-density polyethylene, the containers resist rust, mildew, and splintering and can be cleaned with soap and water.

By thinking in circles, Deere has eliminated 1,200 truckloads of non-recyclable corrugated cardboard going to landfills annually.[11] Disposal costs translated into bottom-line savings of approximately $1.5 million in 1995.[12]

Go with the Flow

Look for opportunities to harness nature's own technologies. This may include using gravity, as Colgate does, to "power" toothpaste tubes or lotions, or using green plants to filter indoor air pollutants. This may also include generating renewable sources of power, such as solar, wind, hydroelectric, or geothermal.

Solar power charges a host of devices ranging from $4 pocket calculators to $10,000 home-energy systems, now used in more than one million U.S. homes. The market for solar-powered appliances and photovoltaic home-energy systems is estimated at $1.5 billion in the United States and has grown 20 percent each year since 1992. Add in biomass, wind, geothermal, and other renewable energy technologies, and the market grows to $3.5 billion.[13] Many utilities, like Traverse City Light and Power, creators of an innovative "Green Rate" wind program, are beginning to notice the possibilities.

 Case Study **The Coming Age of Renewable Power**

"Green pricing" is catching on at electric power utilities across the nation. This refers to programs through which customers voluntarily pay a premium for electricity generated by renewable resources. Traverse City Light and Power, a municipal utility in Michigan, offers one of the most successful of such programs.

Under the plan, called "Green Rate," customers pay a 1.58¢-per-kilowatt-hour premium for wind power generated by a locally installed Vestas V-44 600-kW wind generator that towers over a local cornfield—the largest operating turbine in the United States.

Customers also agree to buy their electricity for a specific number of years—three years for residential, ten years for commercial customers. Customers are rewarded with locked-in rates—a benefit that can be offered since wind power is not subject to variable fuel costs. To date, 20 commercial customers and 245 residential customers (representing about 3 percent of the utility's patronage) have signed on despite the 17–23 percent premium, depending upon the rate class.[14]

To generate this kind of innovative thinking in your own company, start with some of the techniques used in the Getting to Zero[SM] process.[15] Distill the essence of your product's or package's function and ask: How would Mother Nature do it? Ask: How does nature protect things? Transport seeds? Get rid of waste? Communicate? Ask: What are some things in nature that are *like* our product or package? Search for some metaphors like banana peels and pea pods that can catalyze creativity. Ask: What would we do differently if, as in nature, landfills were not an option?

The next time you want to brainstorm, take your team to the woods instead of a sterile hotel room. Send your colleagues outdoors in search of innovative natural products and packages that are compatible with Earth. Take along some ecologists and biologists.

When taking these steps, keep in mind that using natural prototypes will not only accelerate your thinking, but it can shave light-years off your test market. After all, Mother Nature has been testing her concepts for over four billion years!

IDEAS FOR ACTION

Ask the following questions to uncover opportunities for innovative and pro-active product greening:

- What would it take for our product/industry to exist in a sustainable society? How could we deliver the same product benefits with zero environmental impact?

- Are there opportunities to offer variations in our product to cater to regional differences in climate, topography, and/or after-use/disposal options?

- Do consumers know how best to use our product so as to minimize environmental impact?

- How do consumers use our products? How can we alter our products to better match their needs and habits and still minimize environmental impact?

- Is the mass market ready for our eco-innovation? Should we pursue a niche distribution strategy?

- How do consumers view our products? Have their assumptions about what is environmentally correct for our product or category changed? What are their current expectations?

- What opportunities exist to impact the entire system of design, manufacturing, distribution, and reuse/disposal in which our product is made? Where are the opportunities to make the biggest environmentally oriented contribution?

- What would we have to do differently in order to achieve zero environmental impact?

- What are the opportunities to offer services as an adjunct or replacement to our products?

  - Can we extend the life of our own or another company's products through technical assistance, repair, maintenance, and/or disposal services?
  - Can we lease our products or make them available for paid sharing by a number of customers?
  - Can we offer the service replacement of our product, *e.g.*, lawn-mowing service as opposed to selling lawnmowers?
  - What are our opportunities to offer information or electronic-based substitutes for material products?

- How can we harness the power of nature as inspiration for green product and service development?

  - Are all of our employees trained in the basic principles of ecology?

– Can we provide opportunities for our employees to interact with nature and professionals—such as ecologists and
biologists—who can stimulate their thinking? (Note: See
Chapter 9 for a discussion of The Natural Step employee
environmental awareness program.)

Notes

1. "Sustainable Product-Services Development," introductory
   notes presented by Ezio Manzini at the Pioneer Industries
   on Sustainable Services workshop organized by the United
   Nations Environmental Programme—Working Group on
   Sustainable Product Development at the International
   Natural Engineers and Scientists Conference, "Challenges
   of Sustainable Development," Amsterdam, August 22–25,
   1996.
2. Young, John, "The New Materialism: a Matter of Policy,"
   World Watch, September/October 1994, p. 31.
3. Tierney, John, "Recycling Is Garbage," New York Times
   Magazine, June 30, 1996, p. 44.
4. Canning, Christine, "The Laundry Detergent Market,"
   Household and Personal Products Industry, April 1996, p. 76.
5. "Juvenile Lunch Kits from Rubbermaid Bring Fun to
   Everyday Lunches," Rubbermaid press release, July 1996,
   p. 1.
6. United Nations Environmental Program—Working Group
   on Sustainable Product Development, correspondence to
   members, January 23, 1997.
7. Brookhart, Beth, "Cotton's Little Red Hen," Farm Journal,
   1991, p. 8.
8. "Organic Cotton Hits the Shelves," In Business, Volume 16,
   Number 3, May/June 1994, p. 21.

9. Davis, John Bremer, "Product Stewardship and the Coming Age of Takeback: What Your Company Can Learn from the Electronics Industry's Experience," Cutter Information Corp., Arlington, Massachusetts, 1996, p. 38 and p. 108.
10. *Ibid.*, p. 39.
11. *BioCycle*, December 1993, p. 26.
12. John Deere Lawn and Grounds Care Division press release, 1996, p. 4.
13. Personal communication with Scott Sklar, executive director, Solar Energy Industries Association, May 28, 1997.
14. Telephone conversation with Steve Smiley, Bay Energy Services, February 18, 1997; and *Green Pricing Newsletter*, Ed Holt, ed., The Regulatory Assistance Project Number 3, April 1996.
15. Getting to Zero is a service mark of J. Ottman Consulting, Inc.

6

How to Communicate Green with Impact

Communicating environmental initiatives offers great rewards. With environmentalism now a core American value, and with an increasing number of individuals assuming personal responsibility for the impact of their consumption, environmental themes can add relevance to advertising, public relations, promotional, and other marketing messages.

Because green-related attributes often enhance overall product quality, environment-related communications can reinforce a product's primary benefits—e.g., low operating cost or convenience—and sometimes they can impart powerful emotional end-benefits and imagery that increase impact and add perceived value.

Green communications can also buff up corporate imagery and ward off legislative threats. Because of these many benefits, the potential for green-focused communications can often secure a boost in product-oriented marketing support from upper management. Environment-oriented communication is not without its challenges, however.

CHALLENGES OF GREEN COMMUNICATION

Environmental benefits can be indirect, intangible, or insignificant to the consumer. For example, consumers cannot see the emissions being spared at the power plant when they use energy-saving appliances. Relatedly, they don't see the space saved in the landfill when they recycle their cans and bottles.

Primary product benefits may be compromised. Although many green products are cheaper, faster, better, smaller, and more convenient or durable, some are more expensive, slower, uglier, or less sanitary. Cloth dinner napkins, for example, may be less wasteful than paper but they can't match the convenience of their disposable counterparts. Mass transportation is cheaper than driving and lets one read, socialize, or snooze, but it comes up short on the flexibility demanded by working parents who must pick up the kids, dinner, and dry-cleaning along a circuitous commute home.

Targets can be elusive. Demographically based markets such as homeowners living in the parched Southwest or new mothers with extra pennies to spend on organically grown baby food are easy to pinpoint through conventional media, but lifestyle-based targets such as wildlife lovers or the chemically sensitive are more elusive.

Communications can be costly. Consumers must be educated on the benefits of new technology. New brand names must be established. Corporate green credentials must be put forth. Such tasks can overwhelm the budgets of start-up companies with stiff demands for research and development costs among other needs.

A backlash can occur. Communications that appear insignificant or insincere often invite criticism from any number of stakeholders; environmentalists sniff out those they perceive to be "greenwashers," and state attorneys general are on the prowl for marketers who make deceptive environmental claims.

While such challenges exist, *not* communicating one's environmentally oriented product initiatives presents its own risks. These include being replaced on the shelf by a competitor with recognized green credentials, and lost opportunities to increase market share among the growing number of green consumers. Moreover, marketers who don't tout their product's greenness may find that consumers assume their products are not environmentally sound.

STRATEGIES FOR SUCCESS

Environmentally oriented communications work best when:

- Green product attributes are obvious, legitimate, and meaningful to a sizable number of consumers.

- A product's environmental benefits are tangible and can be clearly and simply communicated.

- Product-related efforts are reinforced by substantive corporate progress.

Use the following strategies to take advantage of the many opportunities afforded by green communications while overcoming the challenges.

EDUCATE

Consumers want to make sure their shopping choices line up with green values, and they are receptive to efforts by marketers to provide them with the information they need to make informed purchasing decisions. For advertisers that make the effort to teach, educational messages provide special opportunities to increase purchase intent, enhance imagery, and bolster credibility. The best educational efforts make environmental benefits tangible through compelling illustrations and statistics.

- To create a market for its Triton paperboard six-pack rings, International Paper first had to educate consumers on the environmental problems their product solves. Reinforced by an attractive visual of ducks, ads explain that conventional six-pack rings can snare fish and waterfowl, whereas Triton six-pack rings are biodegradable, "turn(ing) to mush after a short time in the wild . . . break down and do not threaten the environment or nature's creatures."

- Hangtags that accompany garments made from Wellman's EcoSpun fiber describe the process by which the product is made and provide compelling eco-stats that help consumers visualize and appreciate the product's environmental story. Shoppers learn that for every pound of EcoSpun fiber, approximately 10 bottles are kept out of landfills, and recycling efforts have kept 4.8 billion bottles out of landfills and saved 1.3 million barrels of oil.

- To educate employees and visitors on the environmentally related benefits of organically grown cotton, Patagonia created an exhibit for its corporate headquarters. Displays focused on such topics as the differences between conventional and organic world views, the history of pesticide production, and the fundamentals of chemical-free farming and manufacturing. Thirty fiberboard panels—each four feet tall by three feet wide—displayed text, diagrams, photographs, illustrations, and statistics. An impassioned letter from Yvon Chouinard, the company founder, explained his decision to switch the company to exclusive use of the more benignly produced fabric. Interactive displays played a tape recording of the traditional "Boll Weevil Song," by Carl Sandberg, while live lacewing bugs gave viewers a chance to experience beneficial insects firsthand.

EMPOWER CONSUMERS WITH SOLUTIONS

Environmentally concerned individuals respond to emotionally driven messages arming them with specific strategies for helping them acquire a sense of control over their lives. Demonstrate how environmentally sound products and services help consumers protect health, preserve the environment for future generations, or protect the outdoors for recreation and wildlife.

- Rather than promising magical transformations in one's outward appearance, The Body Shop retail cosmetics chain empowers its socially conscious audience to "Make up your mind, not just your face." Advertising messages shun discussions of product superiority and idealized images of glamorous users. Headlines exclaim "Humanism, enthusiasm, love, intuition, curiosity, humor, magic, and fun. You can bottle it! And recycle it!" Window displays and in-store literature showcase environmental causes such as ozone layer depletion and global warming—not artsy product promotions.

- Ads for Working Assets long-distance telephone services, which directs 1 percent of its customers' phone charges to nonprofit organizations such as Greenpeace, Rocky Mountain Institute, Natural Resources Defense Council, and American Rivers, empowers customers to "build a better world just by talking on the phone." Acknowledging that the socially aware are a growing niche in the marketplace and that people are becoming more concerned about letting their money speak for them, Working Assets appeals to those who favor peace, human rights, economic justice, and a safer environment.

Recognizing the activist nature of its customers, Working Assets provides Free Speech days, allowing members to make free calls to senators to support legislation and other issues, and offers to send a Citizen Letter to targeted decisionmakers for a small fee. In 1995 alone, Working Assets customers contacted key political and social leaders nearly one million times, becoming a very powerful citizens' group. Their integration of social responsibility and long-distance service has been so successful that they are branching the concept out into new products and services such as Internet access, business long distance, and Working Assets credit cards.

- In a pilot of electric utility deregulation in New Hampshire, Green Mountain Energy Partners reinforces the promise of its largely hydroelectric power program to rid the air of nasty pollutants by offering consumers a free sapling. Consumers who send in a picture of themselves beside the planted sapling receive "Eco-credits," good toward purchases from the Seventh Generation and Gardener's Choice catalogs.

- The U.K. government's million-dollar ad campaign to fight global warming invited the public to "Switch off your kettle to save the world." Prompted by animated cartoons of steaming kettles and globes in greenhouses, hundreds of thousands of consumers called a government hotline seeking more information. A linked "Helping the Earth" Week attracted support from companies, local governments, and charities.

Notes David Jones, chief executive of the London ad agency Collett Dickinson Pearce on his work's effectiveness, "The child's perspective helps us to bring home to adults that these issues are about their children's future. At the same time, we know that while people are willing to do something, it must not cost much or be too complicated or time consuming."[1]

Be upbeat and positive. Jimmy Carter's campaign for energy conservation failed because of its link to deprivation, which was symbolized in one piece of clothing—a cardigan sweater donned to offset the chill imposed by a lowered thermostat. Like the entire "back to basics" green movement of which it was a part, his well-intended initiative failed because it represented a threat to the upward mobility and prosperity that is America. While some, and the Voluntary Simplifiers in particular (see Chapter 2), may question the idea that "bigger is better" and "growth is necessary for a healthy economy," most Americans are not willing to reverse their hard-won struggle to "have" for a future characterized by "have not." They hope technology coupled with cooperative efforts on the parts of all key players in society will safeguard their future.

So, invite consumers' participation via simple actions, not by leveraging fear tactics, playing to pessimism, or pressing guilt buttons.

- Green Disk of Preston, Washington, manufacturers of computer diskettes that are recaptured from unsold, unopened packages of software, plants lighthearted messages on the bottom of their packages like "Good Planets are Hard to Find" and "100% Re-Made in America."

Use highly illustrative visuals to strengthen the upbeat emotional appeal of environmental advertising. Research conducted by Roper Starch Worldwide and Competitive Media on more than 300 green ads that appeared in 186 magazines between 1991 and 1995 turned up three worthy notes of advice:

- Exploit the inherent visual power in environmentalism. Make illustrations big, bright, and beautiful. If possible, have them bleed off the page. And, when appropriate, give them some drama—something to make them connect with the human heart.

- In general, being specific is better than being general. A close-up shot of a spotted owl looking all feathery and cute or a nest of little owls will be far more effective in drawing a crowd than a chart showing the birds' probable demise and extinction.

- Take a stand and state it powerfully. Most Americans favor, at least in principle, the prospect of a healthier environment; moreover, a significant number of people feel very strongly about environmental issues. It makes little sense, therefore, to mute your environmental message. People respond to powerful statements they agree with and will become more involved with your advertising if their attention is captured by headline and copy that loudly bespeak a strong commitment.[2]

Address the underlying motivations of your target. Empower the disenfranchised. Reward those consumers who are trying to make a difference.

- Motivate True-Blue Greens by demonstrating how they can make a contribution. Reward their initiative, leadership, and commitment.

- Show Greenbacks that environmental benefits are consistent with busy lifestyles and thus add value to products.

- Encourage Sprouts with appeals to fitting in with others in society, status, and doing the right thing.

- Provide Grousers with easy, cost-effective ways to make a contribution.

- Help Basic Browns understand how individuals can make a difference. Underscore that small actions performed by many people can make big changes.

The potential to motivate the large mass of passive greens with the promise of fitting in to society cannot be overstated. That's because environmental issues are inherently social: your gas-guzzling car pollutes my air; my wastefulness clogs our landfill. Today, the "cool" people care about the environment—the influentials, whom many emulate. This dynamic underpinned the most successful anti-litter campaign in history. It was created for the Texas Department of Transportation by the Austin-based GSD&M advertising agency in 1985 and is still running. When research showed that slogans like "Pitch-In" were having no effect on habitual litterers (men 18–34), advertising enlisted popular Texas celebrities like Willie Nelson, Randy White, and George Foreman to demonstrate that it is "uncool" to litter. The "Don't Mess with Texas" campaign has helped to reduce visible roadside litter by 72 percent, saving taxpayers over $2 million per year in cleanup costs.[3]

APPEAL TO CONSUMERS' SELF-INTEREST

Environmentally preferable products like recycled paper and organically grown cotton benefit everybody in society, not just the people who pay the premium to buy them. Reward purchasers for their altruism—and help them over the premium price hump—by demonstrating how environmentally sound products help protect their health, save money, or keep their homes and communities safe and clean. Show busy consumers how some environmentally inclined behaviors can save time and effort. Offer consumers the dual opportunities of saving money or trouble *and* saving the planet, and you've got the stuff for a meaningful sale.

Not surprisingly, such product categories as organically grown food and clothing and compact detergents, where consumers are able to make a connection between the environment and their own personal well-being, are growing faster than categories where people can't immediately experience the benefits.

- An on-package flag for Colgate-Palmolive's "cartonless" stand-up toothpaste tube highlights the benefits to its mass-consumer base with the motivating, "New, Clean and Easy Stand-Up Tube," while an environmentally oriented message is carried on the back. A greener package? Yes, but given the mass audience of the product, the broader message is judged to be more appropriate.

- Advertising for 3M's Scotch Brite Never Rust Soap Pads—made from 100 percent recycled plastic—highlight in-use consumer benefits while the package's side panel details the product's and package's environment-related attributes.

- When introducing its Renewal brand reusable alkaline batteries, Rayovac appealed to heavy battery users with a money-saving benefit. Headlines promised, "How to save $150 on a CD player that costs $100." A supplemental ad campaign announced the number of batteries spared from landfills each year, and complements the potential to save money, "How to save 147 batteries from going to landfills." Sustaining ads use Michael Jordan to underscore the power of Renewal: "More Power," "More Music," and "More Game Time," while a supplemental campaign underscores Renewal's potential to create less waste and protect the environment for future generations.

- In a subtle reference to product performance, ads for ASKO water-saving washing machines assert, "The only thing our washer will shrink is your water bill." Other ads position ASKO washers as: "Stingy with your water. Stingy with your electricity. Stingy with your detergent."

- Tipped off by consumer focus groups, introductory advertising for Procter & Gamble's Downy concentrated fabric softener refill included an appeal to cutting down on waste in addition to what was originally intended as a money-saving-only message. The end result: highly motivating advertising epitomized by the memorable headline of "Put a little more money in your pocket and a little less in your garbage." The U.S. Environmental Protection Agency's tagline for its ENERGY STAR logo also uses an effective dual-benefit message. It reads, "Saving the Planet. Saving your Money."

- In a Washington, D.C., test market for the U.S. Department of Energy's "Energy Saver" label for major appliances, salespeople at Sears, Wards, and Circuit City translated energy efficiency into money-saving data and easy-to-understand equivalencies, such as the number of free loads of laundry. In a follow-up poll, "energy efficiency" rose from seventh or eighth place to second place among shoppers as a key purchasing criteria.[4]

PROVIDE PERFORMANCE REASSURANCE

Environmentally preferable technologies often look or perform differently and may be perceived as less effective than their more familiar brown counterparts. Remove this potential barrier to purchase by addressing the issue head on.

- To counter any lingering sentiment about the inferior quality of products made with recycled content, product labels on Eco-Sleep pillows made from soda-bottle-based fiberfill include the phrase "100% purified."

- To underscore the reliability of its remanufactured copiers, Europe's Rank Xerox markets its machines as "proven workhorses."

- Green Disk backs up their quality with a lifetime guarantee and assurances that diskettes are "triple tested and 100% error free." Advertising lightheartedly reassures customers, "made from the best disks everyone else ever made."

- To make sure that consumers don't think Triton biodegradable six-pack rings will decompose while carrying Coke to the picnic, body copy includes the reassuring note, "They've passed every environmental test; yet they're strong on the job."

CONSIDER A MIX OF MEDIA

While advertising is usually the preferred form of communicating with mass consumers, many green marketers prefer to use alternative media—and it's not just for lack of big budgets. Alternative messages, especially those delivered through non-paid media, can be more credible, as well as capable of reaching green consumers where and when they seek information.

Paid advertising, while capable of reaching mass as well as niche consumers efficiently, may be less than credible for bearing environment-related messages. For instance, Roper has found that advertising receives only moderate support from the True-Blue Greens, the most sophisticated group of environmental consumers. They prefer messages conveyed on packages or through direct marketing and community programs.[5] This finding is corroborated by other researchers, who found that ads had no significant impact on people who were highly involved in the environment.[6]

Green marketers typically rely heavily on public relations tactics to communicate their messages. Companies with a mass target—and who can afford to—use advertising to highlight a brand's primary benefits, while folding in public relations messages to communicate supplemental environmental benefits. The value of this approach is threefold: its public relations efforts target green consumers in a cost-efficient way; it provides third-party credibility; and it reduces the potential for backlash for what might appear to be a self-congratulatory message.

Deep-green companies, including The Body Shop, Ben & Jerry's Homemade, and Stonyfield Farm, have built their corporate reputations and continue to establish goodwill through such creative publicity-generating efforts as adopting local charities, protecting small dairy farmers, and donating profits to charity. Such efforts can build awareness credibly and affordably.

Packaging, the Internet, and company-disseminated information are also excellent green communications vehicles.

A plurality of consumers now claim to read labels to see if products are safer for the environment, and recycling-oriented messages on packaging such as the well-recognized "chasing arrows" symbols on packaging are especially popular.

With a projected 25 million American users by 2000, the World Wide Web represents an efficient means of reaching consumers with information and advice on green products. Environmentalists have long staked out sites on the Internet to share information on global environmental problems, and a few sites now have sub-sites where consumers can obtain information on green products, green companies, and green behavior. Examples include Enviro-Link, Green Market, Eco Expo Online, and EcoMall.

A popular place where consumers look for information is the companies themselves. Procter & Gamble, for one, receives 50,000 environment-related calls each year[7] and growing numbers of consumers access corporate websites. Recognizing that the most active and influential consumers are apt to call or "visit," successful green marketers offer toll-free consumer hotlines as well as attractive information-intensive websites and welcome specific environmentally related questions about their products. Many companies use the opportunity to educate callers with in-depth follow-up literature on their corporate environmental policies and programs. Such deep-green-product companies and catalogs as Seventh Generation and Real Goods have made it an integral part of their strategy to provide extensive education and information for consumers on environment-related product and packaging issues.

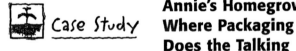 **Case Study** **Annie's Homegrown: Where Packaging Does the Talking**

Ann Withey, owner of Annie's Homegrown, Inc., makers of all-natural macaroni and cheese, lets the packaging do most of the talking for her. Offers for "Be Green" bumper stickers and refrigerator magnets encourage shoppers to pick up the product, write in, and help spread the company's environmentally conscious message. So far, 29,391 people have requested a bumper sticker and 11,585 have ordered the magnets.

Each package sports a signed letter from Annie letting customers know "there is a real Annie," along with, surprisingly enough, Annie's home number. (Annie personally writes back to 25 customers a week and sends form letters to the rest. In addition, Annie fields about 50 calls a day from her Connecticut farm.)

Annie's Homegrown induces word-of-mouth marketing by offering to send discount coupons to customers' friends. The package also sports an Internet website address, allowing the company to communicate in depth with hundreds of other potential customers and route electronic mail messages.

Annie's Homegrown now has a valuable database of 25,000 customer names as well as a $3.5-million business.[8]

IDEAS FOR ACTION

Ask the following questions to evaluate opportunities to add impact to your environmental communications:

- Do our products empower consumers to solve environmental problems? Do they save energy? Conserve water? Cut down on toxics in the waste system?

- Are the environmentally related benefits of our products well understood by our consumers? To which consumers would our product's environmentally oriented benefits appeal most?

- Do our environmental product initiatives represent any direct, tangible benefits to consumers? For instance, do they help consumers save money? Save time? Protect health? Enhance self-esteem?

- Do we need to reassure consumers about our product quality?

- Can we take advantage of opportunities to generate free publicity? Reach consumers on the World Wide Web? Use our package to increase shelf impact and reinforce brand imagery?

Notes

1. Strid, Steve, and Nick Cater, "No Free Ride for Eco-Ads," *Tomorrow*, Volume III, Number 2, 1993, p. 47.
2. Sawyer, Philip W., ed., "It's Not Easy Being Green. How to Improve Advertising with Environmental Themes," *Starch Tested Copy*, Volume 5, Number 2, 1993, p. 5.
3. Personal correspondence with Glenda Goehrs, GSD&M Advertising, December 9, 1996.
4. Makower, Joel, ed., "Seal of Approval," *The Green Business Letter*, Tilden Press, February 1996, p. 2.
5. The Public Pulse newsletter, Roper Starch Worldwide, March 1994, p. 3.
6. Schuwerk and Lefkoff-Higgins, "Green or Non-Green? Does Type of Appeal Matter When Advertising a Green Product?" *Journal of Advertising*, Volume 14, Number 2, 1995, pp. 45–54.
7. "An Environmental Affair," *Household and Personal Products* magazine, December 1995, p. 46.
8. "Let Your Packaging Do the Talking," *Inc.* magazine, July 1996, p. 88.

7

The Secret to
Avoiding Backlash

Even for the most thoroughly researched communications, establishing credibility and avoiding possible backlash is a highly challenging feat. Representing one of the most significant obstacles of green marketing, unanticipated criticism can emanate from many sources, including regulators, environmentalists, the media, consumers, competitors, and the scientific community. Unsuspecting marketers can run afoul of inconsistent state environmental-marketing laws. They can butt up against advocacy groups who question the right of former polluters to tout green credentials of any kind, and they can unintentionally create skeptical consumers among a general public short on facts.

Other credibility hurdles exist, too. Industry suffers from a well-publicized track record of oil spills, Superfund sites, and any number of industrial accidents and health and safety transgressions. And, despite initiatives such as environmental reports, corporate green ads, and new products, consumers believe that industry is still not doing its fair share to clean up the mess. For example, in a random survey of more than 1,000 adults conducted in 1995, 61 percent of respondents agreed that U.S. firms are "much more" or "somewhat more" responsible than they were five years ago, but 55 percent of the respondents believed companies are doing "somewhat less" or "much less" than they should, compared with only 15 percent who felt they are doing more than they should.[1]

Finally, consumers perceive that it is not in industry's interest to promote environmental conservation or decrease consumption; the prevailing economic paradigm, of course, is "growth equals profits." Planned obsolescence was invented by industry to ensure growth; advertising makes consumers want what they do not need. In the words of one environmentalist:

> But all the 50 *Simple Things* (a book on consumer-directed environmental tips) in the world aren't going to make an appreciable dent in our resource abuse until some meaningful changes occur in behavior and lifestyle. And this is where green marketing generally falls on its face: it will never disclose the full range of options. The recycled paper towel package will never shout "Go buy a sponge!" The ozone-friendly Gillette shaving cream can will never advise green consumers to switch to a shaving bar. Green marketing will never offer a well-rounded "third E" (referring to the role of industry in Educating consumers on how to solve environmental ills).[2] (Note: The first two "E"s refer to making it Easy for consumers to buy green products and Empowering consumers to act.)

So it is not surprising that industry's environment-related communications suffer from low credibility, and the potential for backlash exists for claims seen as overcongratulatory or misleading. While credibility is generally higher for corporate ads, only 30 percent of consumers believe ads that say a product is better for the environment than its competitors.[3]

In many cases, backlash cannot be avoided. No company and no product can ever be truly green. Corporate efforts hinting at such aspirations or suggestions will often find detractors. And warm-hearted depictions of furry animals that strike emotional chords with consumers may simultaneously incite the wrath of environmentalists. Pick your target, aim to please *them*, and follow the strategies discussed below to establish credibility and minimize the potential for backlash.

POSITION GREEN PRODUCTS AND PROGRAMS AS PART OF A CORPORATE POLICY OF ENVIRONMENTAL EXCELLENCE

Companies that operate within sound environmental policies need not apologize for failure to achieve perfection. Consumers understand that the greenest of cars will still pollute, the simplest of packaging eventually needs to be thrown away, and the most energy-stingy lightbulbs burn their share of coal and oil at the power plant. Win respect by making progress toward worthy goals, communicating substantively, and, in general, responding positively to the public's concerns and expectations.

- The Chemical Manufacturers Association's (CMA) "Responsible Care" advertising campaign explains that "Since 1987, we've cut the amount of waste we release to water by 56 percent. Clearly, we're only partway there." For added credibility, the CMA advertisement includes a toll-free number to help consumers track the progress of chemical companies in their area and find needed answers. The advertising states, "We want you to know."

- An announcement explaining Apple's move to unbleached fiberboard shipping cartons explained:

  Apple is committed to being environmentally responsible. Changing our box color from white to brown is one step we've taken to reduce pollution and increase the use of recycled materials. Over the coming

months and years, you can expect to see more
progress as we continue to discover ways to care for
the environment. For more information, please contact the Apple Customer Assistance Center at 1-800-
776-2333.

- A memorable headline for an ad detailing Nissan's corporate
  environmental activities declared, "Since we can't live without the car, we better make a car we can live with."

PROMOTE RESPONSIBLE CONSUMPTION

Most Americans intuitively understand that it is not possible to
spend our way out of our environmental crisis. At the micro level,
simply switching one supermarket cartful of "brown" products with
"green" ones will not quash environmental ills. Creating a sustainable society requires—among other things—that every one of
us simply use less; companies that suggest otherwise put themselves
at risk. Win your consumers' respect by articulating the need for
responsible consumption publicly, while making it easy for your
consumers to eat lower on the food chain, generate energy from
renewable resources, or minimize use of raw materials.

- In 1990, Esprit ran ads headlined: "A Plea for Responsible
  Consumption," and asking consumers "(not to) buy any-
  thing you don't need, including our products." Although the
  ad ran on only a limited basis, the company received hundreds of letters from consumers as young as eight years old
  lauding the effort.

- Ads for Danka Industries of St. Petersburg, makers of copier
  and fax machines, encourage consumers to "Recycle at
  Work. Make a World of Difference." Views of nature and
  environmentally responsive workplaces are depicted as
  Danka acknowledges "Waste at Work" and its own efforts to

be part of the solution, including distributing recycling bins and information to employees and customers.[4]

- To help offset future emissions, Chevrolet plants one tree for every Geo sold.

CONSIDER THE ENVIRONMENTAL IMPACT OF YOUR MARKETING METHODS

Environmentally conscious consumers scrutinize the medium in which eco-messages are placed. How many readers looked to see if this book was printed on recycled paper? Use media vehicles that use recycled paper, soybean inks, and are recyclable, or better yet, electronic. Some companies even go so far as to issue only "virtual" press releases and environmental reports.

Apple Computer's carton insert, appropriately, was printed on unbleached recycled-content paper. Recognizing the environmental impact of its direct-mail solicitations, Working Assets uses only recycled paper, and figures out how many trees are used for each mailing and plant more. Many direct-mail catalogs let customers specify how many catalogs they want to receive each year.

USE MEANINGFUL CLAIMS

Commonly used environmental marketing terms can easily mislead unsuspecting consumers. For example, products or packaging made from recycled content can be crafted from 10 percent recycled content or 100 percent recycled content. Recycled content can include "pre-consumer" recycled material such as factory trimmings, or "post-consumer" content such as used milk bottles and newspapers. A package may be recyclable in theory, but collection facilities may not be available to consumers in their communities.

Fortunately, help is available in the form of voluntary guidelines for environmental marketing terms issued by the Federal

Trade Commission (FTC) in 1992 and updated in 1996. (See Appendix.) They include specific recommendations for the most commonly used terms including "recycled," "ozone friendly," "recyclable," "environmentally friendly," "compostable," and "degradable." With some exceptions, individual states including California, Rhode Island, and New York, which had previously passed labeling laws that were inconsistent with the FTC guidelines, have since aligned with the guidelines.

It is now easier for marketers of many types of nationally distributed products to promote environment-related attributes. Indeed, tracking research conducted by researchers at the Universities of Utah and Illinois shows the overall number of product or package claims found in five successive audits of a typical basketful of supermarket products increased 21 percent between 1992 and 1995. In addition, formerly questionable claims such as those relating to plastic trash bag degradability have all but disappeared, as have unqualified claims of "ozone—or environmentally friendly."[5]

A word of caution. While the climate for making environmental claims is sunnier at the end of the 1990s than it was at the start, the coast is still not clear. The potential to confuse and mislead consumers still exists, as does the possibility for crafty competitors to steal unfair advantage.

Considerable debate continues over the use of some individual claims. For instance, the packaging industry argues that an exhortatory claim such as "Please Recycle" on the side of a Pepsi can is an expression of free speech and should be allowed in order to keep up the positive recycling momentum. Regulators aren't so sure.

The 1996 FTC guidelines advise specifically disclosing the limited availability of recycling programs for the material specified, in addition to stating whether the chasing arrows imply recycled or recyclable. They fear that unqualified claims, including the chasing arrows, may mislead consumers into thinking that many packages made from entirely recycled material may be recyclable in their communities when they may not be. This would cause unnecessary burdens for local recyclers stuck with unwanted material and consumers turned off by the apparent deception. On another front, aerosol manufacturers want to fight lingering perceptions that their packages are propelled with chlorofluorocarbons. The FTC fears that a "No CFCs" claim would suggest to consumers that the alternative propellant, hydrofluorocarbon, is environmentally benign.

If your products could be considered "non-toxic," "natural," "water-efficient," "reusable," or "designed for disassembly," you may be out of luck. The FTC has yet to offer use guidelines for these and other terms. Indeed, with "green" constantly evolving, marketers' desire to make safe claims may always be one step ahead of government's ability to respond. To help reduce the risk of confusing or misleading consumers, solicit proper legal counsel and use the following sub-strategies as a guide.

Be Specific and Prominent

Marketers are liable for what consumers may incorrectly interpret as well as what they correctly take away. Prevent deception with the use of simple, crystal-clear language, and be sure to distinguish between product and package. The Wheaties box on your breakfast table likely carries the three chasing arrows symbol with an accompanying claim, "Carton made from 100 percent recycled paperboard. Minimum 35 percent post-consumer content." This claim is specific, and because it qualifies the exact amount of recycled materials, it prevents people from thinking the box is made of 100 percent materials collected at curbside, or is fully recyclable.

Don't play games with type size or proximity of the claim to its qualifiers. Packages heralding Hefty's questionable "photodegradable" trash bag claim had a large "degradable" moniker emblazoned across the package front, while the qualifier, "when exposed to the elements" was placed in small print on the bottom of the front panel.

Provide Complete Information

When comparing your product's environmental benefits to those of a competitor, provide enough information so that consumers can make relevant decisions. Make sure the basis for comparison is sufficiently clear and is substantiated by scientific test results. A claim such as "This shampoo bottle contains 20 percent more recycled content than our previous package" is preferable to the more ambiguous "This shampoo bottle contains 20 percent more recycled content."

Do Not Overstate

Safe Brands of Omaha, Nebraska, learned this lesson the hard way. They ran into legal trouble in 1993 when they attempted to market their Sierra Anti-Freeze/Coolant as "essentially non-toxic" and "biodegradable." Emotionally appealing advertising heralded "It's not just anti-freeze, it's safety freeze . . . safer for kids, pets, and wildlife in the environment." Such claims were based on the fact that Sierra anti-freeze is made with propylene glycol, while other coolants contain ethylene glycol. The problem was that propylene glycol, although less toxic in absolute terms, still poses a hazard to pets and small children. By marketing Sierra as "safe," Safe Brands took the risk that consumers would be less cautious with a hazardous product. In addition, the "biodegradability" claim was essentially meaningless since *all* anti-freeze is biodegradable.

Agitated by the prospect of losing business to a frisky competitor, First Brands Corporation, makers of Prestone, filed a false-advertising lawsuit that was eventually settled out of court. Safe Brands has since changed its claims, and although they boast about a "less toxic" anti-freeze, the claims of "safety-freeze" and "biodegradability" are absent.[6]

Avoid vague, trivial, or irrelevant claims that can create a false impression of a product's or package's overall soundness. Broad labels such as "environmentally safe" or "ozone friendly," if used at all, should be qualified to prevent consumer deception about the specific nature of the environmental benefit being asserted. Preferable alternatives include "This wrapper is environmentally friendly because it was not bleached with chlorine, a process that has been shown to create harmful substances."

Qualify terms such as "energy-efficient," "compostable," "recyclable," "made from recycled content," "refillable," and "reusable." Answer questions such as: How much? For how long? By whom? Where? Compared to what?

Similar rules apply for corporate advertising. Consumers understand that even the most well-intentioned companies still use resources and create waste. Overstating the environmental benefits of one's efforts—wrapping one's company in a green cloak—creates skepticism and invites backlash. Describe where you were before environmental improvements were made. Err on the side of understatement. Also, avoid generalities or sweeping statements such as "We care about the environment" with no connection to projects you have undertaken. Quantify plans, progress, and results. For example, if you announce that your company prevents pollution, explain what kind of pollution and how much. Describe the specific emissions-reduction steps taken both internally and vis-à-vis specific products.

- Panasonic, a division of Matsushita Electric, demonstrates its contribution to environmental protection with corporate ads that talk about how global R&D and manufacturing facilities develop sophisticated technologies like sensors that assist scientists in evaluating ozone layer destruction. Ads also talk about innovations in consumer products, such as dry-cell batteries and fluorescent light-bulbs that lower energy consumption, require fewer resources to manufacture, and are easier to recycle. The headline reads, "There's a lot of talk about saving the ozone layer. We're doing something about it."

Tell the whole story. Decide for yourself: Do you take issue with the fact that advertising conducted by the U.S. Council on Energy

Awareness touts the clean-air benefits of nuclear energy but doesn't mention the radioactive waste it generates? Or that Chevron's long-running "People Do" campaign highlights initiatives that may be required by law? Or that the Chemical Manufacturers Association runs ads citing its industry's attempts to reduce emissions while backing legislation to reduce or eliminate the Toxic Release Inventory, a public database of corporate reports on which and how much of 650 toxic chemicals are being released into plant communities?[7] To be certain that your ads or other environmental communications do not confuse or mislead the consumer, test all messages among your target first.

It pays to be specific. Researchers at San Diego State University found that environmental claims perceived as specific and information-rich fostered positive perceptions of the product as well as the advertiser. They were also more likely to be persuasive than claims perceived as vague, and to lead to higher levels of purchase intent.[8]

Research conducted at Clemson University discovered that, counterintuitively, the more "expert" the judge, the less likely were claims to be found misleading/deceptive. This suggests that better-educated, well-informed consumers may be less skeptical or more receptive to green-oriented advertising, provided it is accurate.[9]

Enlist the Support of Third Parties

When it comes to environment-related messages, the American public believes just about any societal group—not-for-profits, the EPA, local government officials, even the press—before businesses large or small. Third parties can help bolster industry's weak credibility.

Third-party support can come in many forms: local regulators, environmental groups, private consulting organizations that perform independent life cycle inventories (as discussed in Chapter 4), and non-government organizations and government bodies that certify claims and award "eco-seals of approval." Roper found that

Exhibit 7.1

Relationship of Perceived Environmental Claim Specificity to Attitudes Toward the Advertiser, the Product, and Purchase Intent

Environmental Advertising Claim Perceived As:

	Specific	Neutral	Vague
Attitude toward advertiser	2.7	3.5	4.4
Overall product	2.7	4.0	5.0
Specific product attributes	2.6	3.6	4.7
Purchase intent	2.3	4.0	5.4

Note: All means based on a 7-point scale where lower values indicate a more positive response.

Source: Davis, Joel J., "Strategies for Environmental Advertising," Journal of Consumer Marketing, *Vol. 10, No. 2, 1993. Chart reprinted with permission*

"having a company or its products endorsed by an environmental cause or organization," was among the most believable types of corporate environmental protection efforts (see Exhibit 7.2).

- A key to the success of the introduction of ARCO's EC-1 gasoline was opening lines of communication with the South Coast Air Quality Management Board. This local regulatory board endorsed ARCO's reformulated gasoline advertising, and, as such, helped to protect ARCO from the wrath of potential skeptics who favored "purer" solutions such as electric cars and alternative fuel vehicles.

- Before announcing Starkist's "Dolphin Safe" policy to the Heinz Board of Directors and the public, Heinz CEO Anthony O'Reilly consulted with David Phillips, executive director of

Exhibit 7.2

How Believable Are Company Efforts to Protect the Environment?

	Very believable	Somewhat	Not very	Not at all
Have a company or its products endorsed by an environmental cause or organization	23%	54%	16%	3%
Donating money to an environmental cause or issue through a foundation or nonprofit organization	21%	55%	17%	3%
Donating a percentage of sales or profits to an environmental cause or issue	21%	54%	18%	3%
Saying that the company is educating the public to take action to help protect the environment through brochures, seminars, videos, or special events	15%	56%	20%	4%
Saying that the company addresses environmental problems through all company policies, from manufacturing products to marketing	14%	48%	28%	6%
Advertisements showing how the company's efforts have made a significant improvement in protecting the environment	13%	61%	19%	3%

Note: In cases where percentage does not total 100, remaining respondents answered "Don't know."

Source: Roper Starch Worldwide, Green Gauge, 1996. Used with permission

the Earth Island Institute, the environmental group that spearheaded the nationwide boycott of tuna canners. Phillips set high standards for Heinz to meet, including a ban on dolphin-unsafe tuna throughout Heinz's operations worldwide. Records of Heinz's compliance had to be open to inspection by Earth Island Institute, and Heinz had to support the Dolphin Protection Consumer Information Act.

- Although they may help to divert empty soda bottles or used paper from landfills, products made from recycled content are not necessarily environmentally superior overall to their virgin counterparts. Acknowledging this, Wellman commissioned an independent organization to conduct a comparative life cycle analysis to help consumers understand that its recycled content EcoSpun fabric also helps to reduce air and water pollution.

In the future, disclosure of product-related environmental impacts and processes could be required by law. Get a jump on competitors and regulators—and score some points with consumers—by promoting as much about your own products *voluntarily*.

- Pitney-Bowes is just one company that boldly touts its ENERGY STAR label on packages, ads, product documentation, and other communications.

Not all third parties are created equal, so if you opt to go this route, choose wisely. Consider your potential partner's credibility, awareness of the seal or group among consumers, and appropriateness of the group or symbol to your target audience and product category.

Consider Eco-Seals

Eco-seals, independent symbols of environmental preferability granted by governments or independent organizations, as well as statements of environmental independent claim certification, have much to offer green marketers, but are not without risk. On the plus side, as the mark of a third party, they can enhance consumer confidence in environmental promises. Because consumers tend to pick up eco-labeled products off the shelf, they represent a cost-effective marketing tool. They can also halo corporate imagery.

At least 25 countries around the world now offer eco-seal programs (see Exhibit 7.3). Most are run by governments who make their awards on the basis of specific environmental attributes of particular relevance to the respective product category, e.g., emissions of volatile organic compounds from paints, or a form of life cycle analysis.

In the United States, aside from the ENERGY STAR certification program for electronic office products and major appliances, the federal government has opted to let the private sector hold sway in the area of general eco-labeling, subject to the same regulations as environmental marketing claims. Indeed, a number of independent programs granting their own eco-seals have sprung up. Should one's product or service meet their specifications, it can bear any number of specific eco-seals including "dolphin-safe," "forest friendly," and even "ecotel," a certification program for hotels.

Green Seal, a not-for-profit group founded in 1990 by a coalition of environmentalists and other interested parties, will provide a seal of approval for products that meet specific criteria on a category by category basis. Companies pay a fee to have their products evaluated and annually monitored. Products that meet or exceed the standards are authorized to display the Green Seal mark on the product and on promotional material. All manufacturers of products in a category are eligible to apply for the Green Seal. The group has finalized standards covering 84 categories including general-purpose cleaners, compact fluorescent lamps, re-refined engine oil, printing and writing papers, water heaters, washers, dryers, and refrigerator/freezers. The United States Postal Service, Carrier, and the Trane Company are just a few of the organizations whose

Exhibit 7.3
Worldwide Eco-Seals

products now bear the Green Seal certification mark—a blue globe with a green check (see Exhibit 7.4).

A second organization, Scientific Certification Systems of Oakland, California, will certify specific claims or provide manufacturers with a detailed "eco-profile" of their product's environmental impact akin to a nutritional label for display on product labels. Companies whose product claims have either been certified or who bear an eco-profile include Wellman, Glidden, and Owens-Corning.

Empirical evidence suggests that independent seals of approval can lend credibility to environmental messages and help to attract business among environmentally conscious consumers. Environmental marketing managers report that the presence of the Green Seal opens the door to conversations with distributors and retailers that might not otherwise have occurred. Markets that are potentially receptive to eco-seals and independent claim certification include government agencies and their contractors looking to procure environmentally conscious goods, retailers anxious to stock green goods but lacking the ability to decide what is "green" for themselves, and consumers in such areas as Germany and Scandinavia, where eco-seals are well established.

Caution: eco-seals are not without controversy. Critics, including many multinational companies, charge that the science upon

---

Exhibit 7.4
Green Seal and Scientific Certification Systems'
Cross and Globe Labels

Source: Logos used with permission from Green Seal and Scientific Certification Systems

which eco-labels are based is too subjective; the specific criteria upon which they are based can limit product innovation; the use of symbols does not educate consumers about the actual environmental attributes of products; and, finally, eco-seal criteria vary from country to country. (Note: Efforts at standardizing the plethora of eco-seals are underway via the European Ecolabel Organization; the International Standards Organization, which is developing general voluntary standards for eco-labeling; and the Global Ecolabelling Network, an international association of eco-labeling programs.) The situation not only creates a logistical nightmare for multinationals, but also raises potential barriers to free trade because criteria are often based on national or regional priorities.[10]

Considering an eco-seal for your product? Maximize its potential value and avoid backlash by sticking to these strategies:

- Choose wisely. Take care to ensure that the organization behind the seal you choose is well respected and its methodologies are accepted by leading environmentalists as well as by others in your industry. Also, try to use seals with as broad a following as possible, or risk desensitizing consumers with a proliferation of labels.

- Educate. Eco-seals in isolation can mislead consumers into thinking that the product that bears the seal is environmentally superior overall. Educate your consumers about the *specific criteria* upon which your eco-seal is based. Also, teach consumers how to use your product responsibly.

- Extend environmentalism to other parts of your company. Logically speaking, greener products spring from greener companies, although this is not always the case. To avoid backlash, make sure your eco-seal or claim certification is backed up with positive corporate achievements. Ideally, like environmental product attributes in general, eco-seals should be positioned as an extension of one's corporate environmental commitment.

- Promote your seal. Considering that individual seals are not widely recognized, enhance their value by promoting them via advertising and other communications efforts.

IDEAS FOR ACTION

Ask the following questions to evaluate opportunities to add credibility to your environmental communications.

- Are our claims consistent with the laws that may exist in the states where we distribute? Are we following guidelines for environmental marketing claims issued by the Federal Trade Commission? Does our company's legal department have its own guidelines for the use of environmental marketing claims?

- Are our claims specific? Have we tested their communication among consumers?

- Should we have our product's environmental benefits certified by a third party?

- Do eco-seals represent an opportunity for our business either in the United States or other countries?

- Are the print media in which we advertise or promote using recycled paper and soy-based inks?

- Do consumers know how to use and dispose of our products responsibly?

- Have we thoroughly considered all that can go wrong so as to minimize the chances of backlash and enjoy the full benefits of positive publicity?

Notes

1. "Public Still Critical of E-Performance," *Environment Today*, September 1995, p. 10.

2. Letter to J. Ottman from Hannah Holmes, associate editor, *Garbage*, March 13, 1992.

3. Roper Starch Worldwide, as quoted in Stisser, Peter A., "A Deeper Shade of Green," *American Demographics*, March 1994, p. 27.

4. "Selected Environmental Advertising Campaigns, 1993," *Green MarketAlert*, Carl Frankel, ed., December 1993, p. 5.

5. Cude, Brenda J., University of Illinois et al., "Trends in Environmental Marketing Claims Since the FTC Guides: Technical Report," May 1, 1995, p. 5.

6. *Green MarketAlert*, Carl Frankel, ed., December 1993, p. 5.

7. Helvarg, David, "The Big Green Spin Machine, Corporations and Environmental PR," *The Amicus Journal*, Summer 1996, p. 15.

8. Davis, Joel J., "Strategies for Environmental Advertising," *Journal of Consumer Marketing*, Volume 10, Number 2, 1993, pp. 23–25. MCB-University Press 0736-3761.

9. Kangun, Norman, Les Carlson, and Stephen J. Grove, Department of Marketing, Clemson University, "Environmental Advertising Claims: a Preliminary Investigation," *Journal of Public Policy and Marketing*, Volume 10, Number 2, Fall 1991, p. 53.

10. Shimp, Robert J., Ph.D., Procter & Gamble Company, "The Reality of Eco-Seals: Barriers to Environmental Progress in the Global Marketplace," delivered at the "Take it Back" conference, May 2–3, 1996, pp. 1–2.

8

Team Up for Success

It used to be that investors, employees, customers, and suppliers were the only ones with a keen interest in a company's activities. However, now that the condition of the ecology is a key issue, eyes from practically every corner of society scrutinize firms' activities with an eye on environmental impact. These new corporate environmental stakeholders include the general public, community activists, lawmakers, educators, church leaders, even children and future generations who will feel the effects of today's corporate activities in decades to come. Like conventional industry stakeholders, they have a direct stake in the environmental- and societal-related activities of specific industries and firms.

Affecting activities as diverse as raw-material procurement, product development, production, and promotion, some groups monitor specific companies' environmental impact with an eye toward shutting down polluting operations; boycotting, conducting negative media campaigns, and lobbying for stiff new laws are tools in their arsenal. A growing number of others, however, are actually looking to contribute positively by engaging individual industries or companies in collaborative efforts. There is much to gain from enlisting their support.

Exhibit 8.1
The New Corporate Environmental Stakeholders

General Public

Retailers

Educators

Environmental and Social Activists

Church Leaders

Regulators and Legislators

Children and Future Generations

Source: J. Ottman Consulting, Inc.

NEW ENVIRONMENTAL STAKEHOLDERS

A growing number of enlightened marketers find that forming constructive partnerships—or coalitions—with willing stakeholder groups provides many positive benefits. These advantages include

- positive dialogue that leads to objectivity

- advance warning of pending changes in regulations

- access to new markets

- opportunities to educate consumers about key environmental issues relating to one's firm and industry

- technical expertise that can help improve the value of existing products, lead to new products, or cut costs

- bolstered credibility for green products and communications

- enhanced image and heightened impact

- positive publicity that can help stretch marketing efforts

An increasing number of people now see the logic in pooling the collective skills, capabilities, and resources of various societal stakeholder groups in solving complex environmental problems. Smart marketers are now staking out their ground among the realm of available partnership opportunities. The much-heralded McDonald's alliance with the Environmental Defense Fund has given other marketers the confidence to forge successful alliances of their own.

Such key corporate environmental stakeholders as the general public, employees, retailers, suppliers, environmental groups, and government each have their own needs and agendas. This chapter details the challenges and opportunities posed by forming alliances with these particular corporate environmental stakeholders, and offers strategies for working positively with them.

GENERAL PUBLIC STAKEHOLDERS

Educating the public on how best to solve environmental problems and establishing favorable perceptions is highly challenging. Individuals lack basic awareness of ecological principles and processes, and the emotionalism inherent in environmental issues, coupled with rampant misperceptions, can make consumers turn their backs on individual companies or industries overnight. The apple industry still reels over extreme public reaction to a public service campaign against the Alar pesticide in 1989.

These same challenges, if not addressed, can stand in the way of industry's ability to secure favorable sites for manufacturing plants, recruit the best employees, and ensure continued markets for their products. Negative attitudes toward aerosols, chemicals, disposable diapers, and what is perceived as excess packaging are just a few examples.

The need to communicate with and educate the general public is made even more urgent when children are brought into the picture. While children represent a force for positive social as well as environmental change—consider their influence in getting parents to buckle up or stop smoking—their influence can also hinder progress. For example, the general public relishes simple solutions to environment-related dilemmas. Idealistic children, armed with a small bit of information can turn into enviro-cops with easy—albeit often incorrect—mandates. Parents be damned! This already seems to be happening with children's influence on recycling activities within the home.

While recycling is a necessary and desirable consumer behavior, it is not the complete answer to reducing landfill disposal problems that many adults and children perceive. Rather than "reduce, reuse, and recycle," the desirable hierarchy for many consumers is more often "recycle, recycle, landfill." As detailed in Exhibit 2.3, at 49 percent, more consumers engage in recycling than any other eco-related activity. Moreover, consumers are much more likely to engage in recycling-related behaviors, such as buying products that can be recycled or products made from recycled content, than in trying to avoid waste in the first place by using refillable containers or buying fewer disposables.

The implications of consumers' blind love for recycling can be significant. Because they were not recyclable, aseptic packages were banned from the state of Maine in 1990. (They were reinstated four years later, when pilot recycling programs were set up and knowledge of their energy and source reduction benefits was established.) Even today, 63 percent of Americans favor stricter recycling laws and 93 percent think manufacturers should be required to design products with a certain percentage of recycled content, even though such design strategies as durability and reduced packaging may represent environmentally superior solutions.[1]

With declining stocks of natural resources, along with household solid waste that is expected to climb to 250.6 million tons by 2010 (see Exhibit 8.2), and a practical limit on the amount of recoverable materials from households estimated at 25–35 percent,[2] consumer attention in the years ahead must be refocused on alternative product designs and materials-use policies as well as on complements to recycling, such as source reduction and composting.

Opportunities to Educate

Clearly, we need a well-informed public equipped to make rational purchasing and policy decisions about such things as products, packaging, and manufacturing processes. Industry has the relevant facts and technical information, not to mention the necessary regulatory and consumer incentives, to help clarify the issues and get the public on a legitimately greener track. Indeed, several corporations and their competitors regularly undertake cooperative communications initiatives to encourage the attitudinal and behavioral changes necessary to support balanced solutions to environmental issues. One example includes an educational campaign conducted by the Aseptic Package Council underscoring the energy and source education benefits of "juice boxes." Beyond mass media campaigns, businesses can enlist the support of such various other stakeholders as educators, employees, and retailers.

EDUCATORS

Educators are willing stakeholder partners. Teachers welcome educational materials to help answer students' environmental questions, and ecology's topical nature helps to lighten up an otherwise dry science, math, or civics lesson. The Consumer Aerosol Products Council (CAPCO), formed in 1991 to correct misperceptions regarding the use of CFCs in aerosols, is just one industry organization that takes advantage of opportunities to ally with teachers in educating children about their products.

In 1995, with only 26 percent of the public aware of the fact that aerosol products do not contain chlorofluorocarbons—and declining sales—CAPCO released an educational program to inform the public how aerosol products work and their impact on the environment.

Created by a team from the popular children's science program "Beakman's World" with input from a Teacher Review Board comprised of middle- and high-school teachers, it uses humor to create a lively instructional program. Available free of charge, "Another Awesome Aerosol Adventure" succeeds the award-winning "The Aerosol Adventure," which has reached nearly 750,000 students across the country since 1991. Geared for students in grades four through eight, the package includes an 11-minute video featuring Can Do Man, "defender of aerosol cans everywhere." Teacher and student workbooks are revised and updated by an organization which has developed educational programs for the American Chemical Society, the 4-H National Council, and the British Department of Education.[3]

Industry-sponsored classroom eco-efforts must be careful to avoid suggestions of bias. For example, a Procter & Gamble–produced teacher's guide entitled "Decision: Earth" focused on life cycle issues associated with such products as soda cans, pizza packaging, and diapers. It was taken to task by Californians Against Waste and other groups. They objected to the materials — and protested their use in California and several other states — because they contained assertions, for example, that disposable diapers are more favorable than cloth; that clear-cutting creates new habitats for wildlife; and that American forests contain more wood than they did four decades ago, despite the destruction of roughly 97 percent of the nation's old-growth forests.[4]

Besides creating school curricula, take advantage of other opportunities that exist to educate students. Sponsor such children's publications and environmentally oriented television programming as Discovery Channel, Network Earth, and Captain Planet. Cooperate with national or local youth groups and sponsor community recycling or cleanup projects. Or create a corporate environmental club, like Wal-Mart and Target Stores have done.

Exhibit 8.2

U.S. Municipal Solid Waste Generation

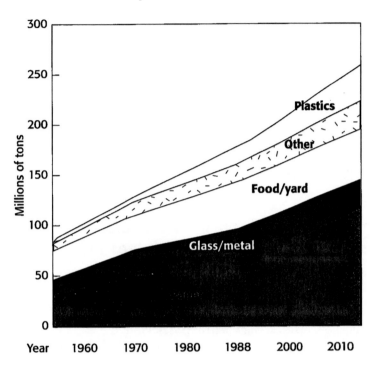

Millions of Tons

	1960	1970	1980	1988	2000	2010
Paper	29.9	44.2	54.7	71.8	96.1	121.2
Glass/metal	17.2	26.8	29.5	27.8	27.2	27.0
Food/yard	33.5	37.8	42.9	47.5	50.6	52.8
Plastics	0.4	3.1	7.8	14.4	21.1	25.7
Other	6.8	10.0	14.7	18.1	21.0	23.9
	87.8	121.9	149.6	179.6	216.0	250.6

Source: U.S. EPA, "Characterization of Municipal Solid Waste in the United States. 1990 Update," Executive Summary, Figure ES-6.

EMPLOYEES

Employees are also able partners in the cause of environment-related education. Employees wear many stakeholder hats. They rely on corporations for their livelihood and have a personal stake in preserving their industry's reputation and markets. As employees, they want to feel good about where they work. Employees are also likely to be members of a corporation's local community as well as purchasers of its products. Enlist their support as the Chemical Specialties Manufacturers Association has — make them liaisons to the community, and of course, to their own families and friends.

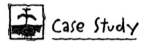 **Chemical Manufacturers Enlist Employees to Help Fight Chemophobia**

The Chem+Life communications program is sponsored by the Chemical Specialties Manufacturers Association (CSMA), the industry that makes many of the chemicals that go into everyday household cleaners, solvents, waxes, and other products. The program counters chemophobia by assisting chemical companies in educating employees about the value of chemical products. Launched in 1993 with an introductory kit containing program messages, suggested experiments, and other informational material to be distributed to employees and others, the goal of the program is to reverse the chemical industry's negative image and inform the public, through employees, of the importance of chemical products in ensuring health, sanitation, and quality of life.

At one participating company, unskilled laborers learn how to decipher chemical data sheets and are counseled on the safe handling of chemicals. At another firm, an aerosol filler uses a scientific experiment to demonstrate that all is not as it seems, especially in the case of aerosol packaging, while employees at a third company learn how to fight chemophobia with the help of an employee newsletter and a coloring book that influences kids and parents alike.

Program participants agree that the message must be clear and simple to be most effective, that demonstrations and meetings are useful, and that, above all, the industry must be honest with employees to build a solid, trusting relationship beneficial to both sides.[5]

RETAILERS

Retailers are another potential source of stakeholder support in educating the general public. Besides being on the front line of consumer demand, retailers have their own environmental issues to manage. Their concerns include source reduction and recycling, energy involved in lighting, heating, air conditioning, and indoor air quality. (Retailers consume about one-sixth of U.S. commercial energy.) At the same time, retailers have direct access to influential green consumers. Teaming up with retailers to educate consumers often brings in-store merchandising support that can boost sales as well as strengthen vendor relationships.

Retailers know that for a variety of reasons including credibility and cost, they need to be green too. Acknowledging the spending power of discriminating green consumers, and desirous of pre-empting legislation while meeting their own employees' demands, many retailers assume a pro-active environmental stance. Grocery stores recycle plastic bags. Many retailers work with vendors to reduce excess packaging, and several, including Target, Home Depot, and The Gap, voluntarily install energy-efficient lighting.

![icon] Case Study   Wal-Mart's New Green Store

Since 1989 when Sam Walton launched retailing's first major environmental marketing program, Wal-Mart has been engaged in myriad environment-related activities. One of the most notable is the building of an entire green store in Lawrence, Kansas, designed to be environmentally sound from the ground up. The store incorporates such features as sustainably harvested wood, a rooftop rainwater-collection system, solar-powered outdoor signage, and a specially designed system of natural "daylighting" that has been linked to increased sales, presumably because of the pleasant environment and the enhanced attractiveness of the merchandise itself.

The store also includes an extensive recycling area and facilities for on-site community education. A second green demonstration store in Industry, California, incorporates high-tech skylights, a massive solar-electric awning that produces 14,000 watts of electricity to light, heat, and cool the building as well as a granite-like interior finishing material made primarily of recycled newsprint and a bio-based resin derived from soy flour.

With major retail chains now developing more comprehensive responses to environmental concerns, the potential to educate is great. Leverage this opportunity by educating retailers on environmental issues, by helping them set up in-store recycling and waste-reduction programs, and by developing green consumer education and promotional programs. One retailer that understands these challenges and opportunities is Home Depot.

 **Case Study**

Home Depot's Environmental Greenprint and Other Initiatives

In the retail home-center industry, Home Depot's financial success is not its only distinguishing factor. The company's strong commitment to environmentalism has won many kudos from consumers, the government, other businesses, and environmentalists. Home Depot set out to address the challenges of being green while meeting the needs of its customers through a variety of programs. The 479-chain store began to seriously incorporate environmentalism into the company in 1990, shortly after the 20th anniversary of Earth Day. As part of its commitment, it published a much-imitated set of Corporate Environmental Principles, and has been empowering its consumers ever since with access to alternative products and reliable environmental claims information. (Simultaneously, the company is protecting itself from liability stemming from consumer confusion associated with any false environmental claims by vendors.)

In 1991, Home Depot became the first major retailer in the United States to successfully establish a third-party evaluation process for environmental claims. In a program with Scientific Certification Systems (SCS), Home Depot requires the verification of all claims made on labels, in-store displays, and advertising published for Home Depot use. The program addresses claims about specific products as well as claims regarding a company's environmental records.

Home Depot's consumer education efforts do not stop there. In 1992, the company began publishing its "Environmental Greenprint" which was distributed in all of its stores. The "Environmental Greenprint" mapped out areas of the home where environmentally sound products and practices can be used and implemented. For example, it recommended the use of light-colored roof shingles, light dimmers, and ceiling fans as energy savers, and faucet aerators and water timers for lawns as water savers. It also included many green home-improvement tips, an environmental checklist for homeowners, and a handy list of contact numbers for more information on related subjects such as lead, pesticides, and energy efficiency.

As an extension of the "Environmental Greenprint" program, Home Depot works in conjunction with Habitat for Humanity, a nonprofit organization designed to incorporate cost-saving, environmentally preferable building material and techniques into homes for underprivileged families. Other pioneering environmental initiatives include encouraging the purchase of simulated wood for hollow-core interior doors instead of tropical hardwoods, discontinuing sales of lead plumbing solder, requiring suppliers to replace wood pallets with reusable slip sheets, and joining the EPA's Green Lights Program.

In 1993, Home Depot also created the industry's first Recycling Depots, which allow customers to sell back recyclables such as old wire, ladders, sinks, and grills. After separating out the various recyclable parts, Home Depot sells the material to partner scrap yards in the community. For customers, the recycling center is a definite plus in that they get cash for old household parts together with the convenience of being able to buy new. According to company estimates, approximately 6.5 million pounds of material have been saved from the landfills as a result of this program.

All these efforts have helped to keep Home Depot among the nation's most admired corporations and in 1996 earned the company, among other accolades, an award from the President's Council on Sustainable Development.[6]

IDEAS FOR ACTION

Ask the following questions to assess opportunities for enlisting consumers', educators', and retailers' support for your company's environment-related initiatives:

- How knowledgeable are our consumers on the environmental issues that affect our industry, company, and products?

- What types of messages do we need to get to consumers about the issues to improve our positioning long term?

- What do consumers need to know in order to use, recycle, and safely dispose of our products and packaging?

- What roles do children play in influencing the purchase of our products?

- What opportunities exist to develop environmental education programs or curricula?

- What other types of programs can we sponsor to reach children with our messages. Community projects? Environmental clubs? Children's media?

- What opportunities exist to enlist our employees' support in getting our message out?

- What are the most important environmental issues facing our key retailers in their trading areas?

- What types of education and training do buyers and sales personnel require about environmental issues for our brand/category?

- To what extent are our retailers aware of our environmental initiatives and the environmentally sound attributes of our products and packaging?

- What are the opportunities for our brand to get enhanced sales and in-store support from the most environmentally aware/concerned retailers?

GOVERNMENT

It used to be a question of "jobs versus the environment," and "loggers versus spotted owls." That was in the days when government's primary tool kit consisted of passing laws that entailed costly "end-of-pipe" cleanup methods, and the concomitant risk of hefty fines. In attempting to comply, some companies were forced out of business or had to scale back operations—and jobs along with them. But things are starting to change.

Government is learning that the historical "command and control" approach to environmental protection cannot solve problems by itself. These days, a light is going off in lawmakers' heads: why not develop voluntary programs that can help industry and the economy as well as the environment? Slowly but surely this enlightened approach is starting to take over, creating opportunities for win-win solutions for businesses willing to shed lingering fears associated with letting government legislators and regulators into the tent. Partnering businesses enjoy increased flexibility in meeting existing laws and regulations as well as access to technical resources that can lead to competitive advantage, new marketing opportunities, and enhanced credibility and public recognition for their environmental efforts.

The time for industry and legislators to join together comes none too soon. The voting public, while not giving up on the need for continued regulation of industry, desires market-based solutions to environmental problems. For example, a poll conducted in 1995 by the Roper organization for *Times Mirror* magazines found that 69 percent of adults surveyed believe that "environmental protection and economic development can work together." Backed by a clear mandate, government is adding some new strategies to its environmental protection arsenal. Many of these pay off in big ways for industry.

Voluntary Partnerships

Enlightened politicians and bureaucrats now create exciting voluntary pollution prevention programs for willing industry partners. A plethora of resulting local, state, and federal programs extend an unbeatable package of incentives for businesses looking to control their own destinies.

Green Star® is a community-based environmental leadership program which demonstrates that businesses using environmentally responsible practices can save money and attract customers.

The program was established in Anchorage, Alaska, in 1990 as a partnership between the Alaska Department of Environmental Conservation, the Anchorage Chamber of Commerce, and the Alaska Center for the Environment. Green Star is now its own non-profit organization and remains the point of contact for other communities, inside and outside Alaska, interested in starting other Green Star programs.

Exhibit 8.3

Alaska's Green Star Program® Logo

Source: Logo used with permission of Green Star

Since 1990, Anchorage's program has inspired new chapters in Fairbanks, Nome, Kenai, and Deadhorse. More than 300 Alaska businesses representing 46,000 employees, including AT&T Alascom, Anchorage Hilton, and Safeway, are now enrolled in the program. There are 10 Green Star chapters in the United States, including Midland, Texas; Kauai, Hawaii; and Spokane, Washington.

Businesses enrolling in the program agree to meet 12 of 18 pollution prevention and energy conservation standards (there are six mandatory standards). Once these standards are achieved, the company submits an application for recognition and the Green Star award. The program then conducts a site visit and reviews the company's efforts to meet the program standards.

Businesses successfully completing the standards are recognized in a variety of ways and receive rights to use the trademarked Green Star name and logo. The program also gives technical assistance to those needing help to complete the standards.

Beyond helping businesses to streamline the auditing process and save money, some programs actually create opportunities for industry to profit from pollution-prevention efforts, and even spur sales of environmentally sound products and technologies. The granddaddy of these is the U.S. Environmental Protection Agency's ENERGY STAR program.

 Case Study

EPA Partners with Industry to Prevent Pollution and Boost Profits

Created by the EPA's Atmospheric Pollution Prevention Division in 1991 to promote energy efficiency, the ENERGY STAR program aims to reduce air pollution and greenhouse gas emissions while helping businesses and consumers save money without sacrifice. Participating companies and such other organizations as hospitals,

Exhibit 8.4

U.S. EPA Green Lights and ENERGY STAR Logos

Source: Logos used with permission of the U.S. Environmental Protection Agency

schools, and universities discover that enlightened energy-efficiency strategies yield new sources of competitive advantage: a cleaned-up environment with increased sales and profits, improved workplaces, and better employee morale and productivity, as well as a shine on their corporate image.

Two different programs make up this unique public-private sector effort. The ENERGY STAR and Green Lights® Buildings program is aimed at enhancing energy efficiency within commercial and industrial buildings, and the ENERGY STAR labeling programs are designed to stimulate the market for energy-efficient office equipment, residential heating and cooling equipment, major appliances, and even new homes.

Partners in the ENERGY STAR and Green Lights Buildings program sign a voluntary Memorandum of Understanding (MOU) and agree to upgrade their facilities with energy-efficient technologies within a specific time period, where profitable. In exchange, EPA provides technical and promotional support, including the use of attractive logos to help organizations implement internal upgrades and obtain recognition for their efforts (see Exhibit 8.4).

To date, more than 2,400 corporations, hospitals, schools, and other organizations have realized a 35 percent rate of return on their investments in energy-efficient lighting technologies. They now save, on average, more than 45 percent on lighting bills and prevent approximately 6.3 billion pounds of carbon dioxide emissions from entering the environment yearly while creating a more pleasant and productive work environment for their employees. Among the Green Lights success stories, Johnson & Johnson has slashed operating costs by $3.6 million per year and the University of Texas M.D. Anderson Cancer Center attributes $225,000 in annual savings to its Green Lights initiatives.

Top managers at The Gap, for example, believe energy-efficient lighting and other internal measures pay off in a more comfortable and healthful workplace for employees, and this in turn leads to a competitive edge. Notes Maria Moyer-Angus, Gap's director of environmental affairs, "Where you gain advantage in the competitive apparel industry is by getting the best and brightest people. We do everything we can to recruit and keep employees." She believes Gap's environmental measures lead to improved air quality and aesthetics, which employees value highly.[7]

Manufacturers of ENERGY STAR labeled products also sign an MOU to voluntarily develop new technologies and enhance their products to meet agreed-upon ENERGY STAR guidelines for energy efficiency. In return, they earn the right to display the ENERGY STAR logo on their products and promotions, and can take advantage of unique new sales opportunities being created as a result of an executive order requiring the Executive Branch to procure high-efficiency products that cut down on operating costs throughout their lifetime. Today, 90 percent of all computers, faxes, and printers on the market are ENERGY STAR–compliant. Among its many participants, Compaq, Pitney-Bowes, and Ricoh have won special ENERGY STAR and Green Lights participation awards for their efforts in the program.

Opportunities for Technical and Financial Support

Need some new product ideas and the money to get them from drafting board to market? Consult your local green bureaucrat. Many government agencies today can provide a ready source of new-product technologies and funding. In the United States, just two possibilities include the Forest Products Laboratory (FPL) and the Alternative Agriculture Commercialization and Research Corporation, facilities of the U.S. Department of Agriculture.

Founded in 1910, the USDA's Forest Products Laboratory in Madison, Wisconsin, is the largest forest products research laboratory in the world. With the goal of improving the use of wood to help conserve and better manage wood resources, lab researchers develop technologies and test prototypes that allow wood residuals to be fed into manufacturing processes, analyze the economic feasibility of these technologies, and help develop standards and codes for the use of recycled products.

The other alternative is the Alternative Agricultural Research and Commercialization Corporation (AARC), a venture capital firm wholly owned by the U.S. government. Created in conjunction with the 1990 Farm Bill, AARC's mission is to stimulate rural economies by supporting markets for industrial uses of agricultural and forestry ("bio-based") products. To date, AARC has invested $28 million in over 60 projects, leveraging a total of $93 million in the process. The recipients of its support include Trailblazer paper made from kenaf by Vision Paper; Shadow Lake, Inc., producers of Citra-Solv cleaner and degreaser made from an extract of orange peel; and Gridcore Systems International.[8]

 Case Study

Gridcore Systems International Benefits from Government Support

While researching alternative building materials, architect Robert Noble discovered spaceboard, a new type of building panel developed by the Forest Products Laboratory. Immediately, he saw the tremendous potential for spaceboard, a material that can be manufactured from various recycled or agricultural fibers, and—due to a honeycomb interior design—is just as strong and several times lighter than conventional fiberboard. He created Gridcore Systems International in 1992 to bring this unique material to market.

Gridcore is now under contract with the Forest Products Laboratory, enjoying an exclusive license to commercialize the technology for a variety of applications, expiring in 2004 (concurrent with patents on spaceboard). Gridcore Systems International, in turn, pays an ongoing royalty to the federal government based on production and sales.

Because of its association with the Forest Products Laboratory, Gridcore was able to get special attention from the AARC, which has made equity investments in Gridcore totaling $1.4 million.

Four years after its founding, Gridcore is a full-scale commercial operation with the capacity to produce 13 million square feet of Gridcore subpanels. This capacity translates into potential yearly revenue of around $10 million, a level of production and marketing that would make the company profitable in 1997.[9]

IDEAS FOR ACTION

Ask the following questions to assess opportunities for enlisting the support of government stakeholders:

- What legislation is in effect or underway on the federal, state, and local levels that will affect our brands and company?

- What steps can we take to promote self-regulation and avoid mandatory regulations?

- What voluntary programs being conducted by the local, state, or federal government can we join to help preempt legislation, and gain advantage and set standards in our industry?

- What opportunities exist to market our participation in voluntary government programs to our consumers and other stakeholders?

ENVIRONMENTAL GROUPS

One of the most pronounced developments among environmental groups since the late 1980s and early 1990s is their growing willingness—and in some cases outright desire—to join together with industry for mutual gain. While extremist groups still undertake such activities as spiking trees in the fight to save the spotted owl, a growing number of once fiercely anti-industry groups are softening their stance. They realize that since businesses control many of the resources and yield much of the power in a market-based economy, joining with them is the best way to clean up the environment, encourage more responsible consumption, and pave the way for a sustainable society.

Some groups such as the Council on Economic Priorities realized early on that positive action could be had by using market-based forces; their *Shopping for a Better World Guide*, a popular guidebook on corporate environmental activities, is one example.

These days, other groups leverage market-based forces too. Previously hostile environmental groups such as the Environmental Defense Fund, which helped engineer a ban on the DDT pesticide in 1972, and Greenpeace, the original "rainbow warriors," realize that working positively with industry can help achieve mutual objectives. For example, Greenpeace's plan for an environmentally sound athletic village complex helped Sydney, Aus-

tralia, win the right to host the Olympics in 2000.[10] Even Green
Seal has turned about. Initially a self-pronounced enviro-cop issuing only hard-to-come-by seals of eco-approval, it now runs the
Green Seal Partners Program, advising corporations and industry
on environmentally preferable product procurement.

Many environmental groups are not only open to entrees from
industry, but they offer creative ways to enlist industry's support.
Develop positive relationships with environmentalists via

- corporate philanthropy

- joint industry/advocacy group alliances

- industry/advocacy group roundtables

- cause-related marketing campaigns

- new product alliances

Corporate Philanthropy

Corporate philanthropy, consisting of deductible gifts made
through a foundation arm, or at least noted as such by a corporation in IRS filings, has historically been an effective marketing and
public relations tool. Donations to charities and the arts, for example, have long helped such major corporations as Mobil, IBM, and
Philip Morris burnish their leadership images and make friends
with society's influentials. Although it has been criticized as a
form of propaganda, environmental giving helps companies to
create awareness among influential environmentalists and eco-
conscious consumers for their corporate environmental efforts. It
also creates more favorable impressions for a company overall.
Eastman Kodak, for example, contributes to environmental causes
including the World Wildlife Fund's Windows on the Wild environmental education program, to which $2.7 million has been
contributed over a six-year period in the form of a "no-strings-
attached" grant.

Tap into consumers' desires to support environmental causes by matching employee donations to popular advocacy groups. Individuals are eager to donate money to environmental groups. According to Roper, 25 percent of adults contribute money to environmental groups from time to time. IBM is just one company that matches employee donations on a dollar-for-dollar basis; 5 percent of all corporate contributions go to environmental causes.[11] Join Earthshare (Washington, D.C.), an employee-giving program like the United Way, which channels money to 43 worthy environmental and conservation groups. Corporate partners include Allstate, Gap, Mattel, Nissan, Sears, and Time Warner. Annual giving is about $8 million per year.[12]

Partner with other companies' philanthropic efforts, with facilitation by not-for-profits. For example, the Conservation Alliance, formed in 1989 as the Outdoor Industry Conservation Alliance, represents a coalition of 36 manufacturers of outerwear and recreational equipment joined together to help protect North America's outdoor recreation areas. Since its founding in 1989, the organization, which includes Patagonia, REI, Northface, and *Outside Magazine* among its members, has given nearly $2 million to conservation groups throughout North America.

Industry and Environmental Group Alliances

Environmental groups are often aware of cutting-edge ideas and technologies that can help industry stay in the forefront of change, reduce costs, and develop new products. Their credibility can help to pave the way for the industry-generated initiatives that result. Representing a sea of change in their orientation, environmentalists can be enlisted as industry consultants. McDonald's discovered the upside benefits of teaming up with environmentalists when they and the Environmental Defense Fund pioneered the now-famous alliance that helped embolden other large corporations and environmental groups to join efforts to achieve mutual goals. That alliance has led to the Paper Task Force.

Case Study

Successful Alliance Between McDonald's and Environmental Defense Fund Leads to Paper Task Force

In 1992, McDonald's allied with the Environmental Defense Fund (EDF) and created a 42-step waste-reduction action plan. Three years later, they reunited with the EDF and together with four other organizations created the Paper Task Force. Composed of McDonald's, Johnson & Johnson, Prudential Insurance Company of America, Time, Inc., and Duke University—representing $2 billion in purchasing power—the Paper Task Force yielded a comprehensive report with several recommendations intended as a road map for corporate purchasing managers who want to minimize the environmental impact of the paper they buy.

The Paper Task Force lived up to its expectations. Prudential and Duke University now reduce their consumption of paper through the use of electronic mail and procurement systems instead of paper-based alternatives. McDonald's incorporates consideration of its paper suppliers' forest-management practices into its annual supplier business-review process, and Time, Inc., plans to survey its suppliers regarding their forest-management practices.[13]

Fred Krupp, EDF president, notes that his organization's approach represents a new, third stage in environmentalism. Krupp argues that if Teddy Roosevelt's conservation movement marked the first stage, and if the second stage reflects efforts to reverse pollution of air, water, and soil spurred by Rachel Carson's publication of *Silent Spring* in 1962, then we are now in a third stage, where "Environmentalists . . . have to help find alternative ways to meet the social needs that lie behind the pesticides and power plants that threaten harm." For Krupp, this translates into finding market-based incentives, such as tying waste-reduction to money savings at McDonald's.

Believes Krupp, "Advocates can stand at the edge of the system and see who can shout the loudest. It's more powerful and constructive to piece together solutions." Krupp's philosophy and market-oriented reputation helped win over his first corporate client. Remembers Shelby Yastrow, general counsel for McDonald's, "I knew they couldn't try to talk us into doing something if it was economically unreasonable. Fred wouldn't come in and ask us to go to Wedgewood china."[14]

Industry and Advocacy Group Roundtables

Representing a growing area in relations between two former adversaries, industry/advocacy group roundtables allow corporate participants to engage in constructive dialogue with environmentalists. Both parties share information to better understand each other's points of view and bring about workable solutions.

One of the most visible of these roundtables is CERES, the Coalition for Environmentally Responsible Economies. A coalition of investor, environmental, and labor groups, CERES encourages member companies to endorse and practice the CERES Principles (a 10-item code of corporate environmental conduct formerly called the Valdez Principles after the Exxon oil spill of March 1989) (see Appendix A).

Companies that endorse the CERES Principles pledge to monitor and improve their behavior in such areas as protecting the biosphere and promoting sustainable use of resources, energy conservation, and safe products and services. Companies must also report on their progress with these pledges. Six Fortune 500 companies—Bethlehem Steel, General Motors, Polaroid, Sun Oil, Arizona Public Service, and H. B. Fuller—have already signed the CERES Principles, along with more than 80 other small and mid-size companies including Timberland, Aveda, and Stonyfield Farm.

While some corporate executives may be fearful of entering into an in-depth relationship such as that involved with endorsing the CERES Principles and disclosing the requisite information, this is not the case at Sun Oil. J. Robert Banks, the company's VP of Health, Environment, and Safety testifies to the benefits, "All I can tell you is after a year's worth of being in partnership [with CERES] we couldn't be happier. It has produced a tremendous amount of value-added to our corporation. We value [CERES] inputs and ideas in the things we're doing. We hadn't had that before. They bring perspectives that are different."[15] Consider signing the CERES Principles. Given growing support among America's corporate elite, they could soon represent de facto standards for corporate environmental reporting.

Cause-Related Marketing Programs

Best known as strategic promotional efforts in which businesses donate a percent of product sales to a not-for-profit group or cause, cause-related marketing allows businesses to make an impact well beyond that associated with just writing a check. With cause-related marketing, everybody wins. Consumers can contribute to favorite environmental programs in their communities with little or no added expense or inconvenience; environmental partners enjoy broadened publicity and the potential to attract new members and financial support; and business sponsors and their retailers and distributors can distinguish themselves in a cluttered marketplace, enhance brand equity, and build sales. No longer viewed as a short-term promotional tactic, all signs point to cause-related marketing as a mature, long-term strategic business practice approached with increasing sophistication by some of the largest companies in America.

Now more than ever, cause-related marketing can tip sales in the sponsor's favor. According to the 1997 Cone/Roper Cause-Related Marketing Trends report, 76 percent of consumers polled by Roper in 1996 said they were likely to switch brands and a similar percentage would switch retailers when price and quality are equal if associated with a good cause, up from 66 percent in 1993.

In addition, the degree of skepticism that exists with cause-related marketing has declined dramatically since the early 1990s. Then, 58 percent of consumers suspected that cause-related marketing was "just for show." But today, only 21 percent of consumers say they wonder "if the company's motives are good" when they evaluate a cause-related marketing campaign.

Not surprisingly, cause-related marketing is no longer practiced just by smaller "green" companies such as Ben & Jerry's, or Millstone Coffee, which conducts regional programs in the Pacific Northwest. Today, giants like MCI, Canon, and General Motors team up with environmental groups such as the Arlington, Virginia–based Nature Conservancy, which offers an attractive menu of cause-related opportunities including licensing the use of the group's name and logo on merchandise and conducting worthwhile educational programs.

Growth in sponsorship dollars underscores corporate America's interest in cause-related marketing. According to the Chicago-based IEG Sponsorship Report, for example, spending on cause-related marketing is expected to reach $600 million in 1996, nearly double the $314 million in sponsorship support just three years earlier.[16] Canon's experience is representative of what sponsors can achieve.

 Case Study **Canon: Where Cause-Related Marketing Reinforces Leadership**

At Canon, a corporate philosophy of "kyosei"—living and working together for the common good—guides the company toward cause-related marketing that reinforces Canon's position as a market and environmental leader.

It began with the Clean Earth Campaign in 1990, which donated $1 to be divided between the National Wildlife Federation and The Nature Conservancy for each Canon toner cartridge returned to the company. The five-year effort resulted in the recycling of several million toner cartridges along with a corresponding donation. The success of the program inspired Canon to deepen and enhance their cause-related marketing efforts.

Among other initiatives, the company now supports "NatureServe," a comprehensive program for sharing with the public The Nature Conservancy's scientific knowledge and expertise on natural resources, and "Expedition into the Parks," a program with the National Parks Foundation to inventory and protect rare plant and animal species found in national parks.

These initiatives help Canon U.S.A., Inc., show its environmental concern to its 9,800 employees in the Americas and serve as a model to other companies. The depth and scope of these efforts allow Canon to promote their participation credibly to all stakeholders via such vehicles as the pbs series Nature and ads in National Geographic.[17]

Follow these success strategies to take maximum advantage of opportunities for cause-related marketing:

- Pick a cause that reflects your company's values and one that employees and customers can get excited about. Also, reinforce brand imagery by creating a thematic mesh between your product's benefits and the particular cause—Arm & Hammer brand baking soda's linkage with the Clean Water Action fund is a good example.

- Choose an organization that is equipped to support your logistical and marketing efforts.

- Partner with an organization in which your company will get adequate attention—such questions of scale are particularly important to smaller companies.

New Product Development

Looking for creative new product technologies? Brainstorm with an environmentalist. It was a resourceful environmentalist who first suggested to Bryan Thomlison, then head of marketing for Church & Dwight's Canadian division, that Arm & Hammer brand baking soda be used as an environmentally preferable cleaning agent. Sales which had been flat for seven years, grew 30 percent in 35 months.[18] This idea, and others that have since been culled through committed relationship-building with environmentalists on Thomlison's extensive database, translates to an estimated $75 million of the company's $500 million sales annually.

The S. C. Johnson Co., makers of Glad and Pledge, are now developing the next generation of products with the environment in mind with a not-for-profit group, Alliance for Environmental Innovation, composed largely of the original McDonald's/EDF waste-education task force. And Amory Lovins of Colorado's Rocky Mountain Institute, an energy think tank based in Snowmass, Colorado, now works with the automotive industry to turn his concept for hyper cars, designed for super-efficient energy use, into reality.

IDEAS FOR ACTION

Ask the following questions to assess opportunities for enlisting the support of environmental groups:

- Which environmental groups can lead us to sustainable approaches to running our business?

- Are our environmental initiatives worthy of receiving special recognition by environmental groups?

- What opportunities exist to initiate positive partnerships with local environmental groups?

- Are there opportunities to enhance perceptions of our corporate and brand images by engaging in a cause-related marketing campaign with an environmental group?

- Which environmentalists can help us develop concepts or technologies for new products?

- What outside resources can we use to aid our green-product development efforts? What opportunities exist to work with environmental groups? Government agencies? Suppliers?

SUPPLIERS

Suppliers are a logical place to turn for support in balancing consumers' environmental demands with primary product benefits. Their vested interest and closeness to their own products and technologies enable them to offer creative ways to reduce the environmental impact of specific products and bring new product innovations to the table. Acknowledging this, S. C. Johnson holds annual Supplier Days. Representatives brief suppliers of ingredients, packaging, and other inputs on the corporation's environmental objectives and progress, and educate them on key developments in the field of life cycle analysis, product stewardship, and other green-product development tools. Outstanding supplier initiatives are shared and rewarded.

McDonald's came to appreciate the value of consulting with suppliers on eco-matters when attempting to reduce the amount of material disposed of by its stores. When asked to replace corrugated cartons with shrink-wrap to protect paper-napkins during shipment, the paper-napkin supplier surprised McDonald's source-reduction team by suggesting a more potent alternative: alter the "dimpling" pattern on the napkins. This seemingly minor alteration enabled the supplier to pack 25 percent more napkins in each box, reducing packaging and shipping costs accordingly.[19]

Sometimes the only way to solve complex environmental problems is by joining with suppliers and others. Ethan Allen happily discovered this when the company turned to Ametek, the supplier of the polypropylene foam sheets used to protect its furniture during shipment. Ametek turned Ethan Allen's need to reduce disposal costs into a win-win-win situation for itself, its customer, and the United Parcel Service.

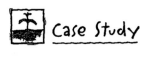 **Case Study** ### Ethan Allen Teams Up with Ametek to Recycle Foam Packaging

To help reduce disposal costs, Ametek, Inc., of Paoli, Pennsylvania, a manufacturer of expanded polypropylene, developed an integrated program for collecting and recycling the foam cushioning used by its customer, Ethan Allen, to protect furniture surfaces during shipment. Ametek pays Ethan Allen 10 cents for each pound of used cushioning shipped back to its facilities for recycling. Shipping is prepaid by Ametek using United Parcel Service's Authorized Return Service, a national package-retrieval program originally developed in 1990 for Canon's toner cartridge-retrieval program.

Since compacting the light, bulky foam is essential, Ethan Allen was required to invest in machines that compact the foam into a dense, easy-to-handle cube averaging eight cubic feet and weighing roughly 55 pounds. UPS provides pre-addressed shipping labels and makes daily pickups, eliminating the need for Ethan Allen to collect and warehouse what would otherwise be a full truckload of material.

Prior to the program, polypropylene waste resulting from Ethan Allen's home-delivery operations filled one eight-yard Dumpster per day on average, costing the company from $600 to $700 per

Dumpster each month to have this material removed for disposal. In this unique recycling program's first year, Ethan Allen home-delivery centers diverted 10,000 pounds of polypropylene foam from landfills.

Since the program was launched, used packaging volume has been reduced by 85 percent and hauling costs have been reduced by 70 percent.[20] This innovative foam-recycling program has helped Ametek strengthen ties to its customer while providing Ametek with a reliable source of clean, used material for recycling into new sheets.[21]

Notes

1. Gallup Poll conducted for Waste Management, Inc., 1995.
2. Recycling Report No. 0185, published by Keep America Beautiful, as quoted in *California Recycling Review*, Summer 1996, p. 3.
3. "Chemical Times and Trends," *CSMA Journal*, October 1995, p. 57.
4. Makower, Joel, ed., *The Green Consumer Letter*, Tilden Press, January 1994, p. 2.
5. "Members Tell How They Use CSMA's Chem+Life Program," *Household and Personal Products Industry* magazine, February 1994, p. 46.
6. Personal communication with Mark Eisen, environmental marketing manager, November 13, 1996.
7. "Minding the Store," *Green Business Letter*, Makower, Joel, ed., February 1996, p. 7.
8. Personal communication with Ron Buckhalt, director of marketing, Alternative Agricultural Research and Commercialization Corporation, February 14, 1997.

9. Steuteville, Robert, "From Laboratory Concept to Real World Sales," *In Business*, November/December 1996, pp. 12–13.

10. "Greenpeace Means Business," *Green Business Letter*, Makower, Joel, ed., 1994, p. 3.

11. "Corporate Environmental Philanthropy," Green MarketAlert, Carl Frankel, ed., October 1993, p. 5.

12. Personal communication with Kalman Stein, executive director, December 9, 1996.

13. "Paper Task Force Offers Paper Purchasing and Use Recommendations," *Business and the Environment*, Cutter Information Corp., January 1996, p. 9.

14. Gutfield, Rose, "Environmental Group Doesn't Always Lick 'Em; It Can Join 'Em and Succeed," *Wall Street Journal*, August 20, 1992, p. B2.

15. "Into the Fast Lane. GM Could Help Make CERES Reporting Vehicle of Choice," *Green Business Letter*, Makower, Joel, ed., March 1994, p. 5.

16. IEG Sponsorship Report, Chicago, 1996. Note: These sponsorship figures do not break out environment-related events per se. However, since 1993, according to the Cone/Roper 1996 survey, support for environment efforts has moved from a fourth priority at the local level to second place as a cause-related focus.

17. Personal communication with Russell Marchetta, July 18, 1997.

18. *Earth Enterprise Tool Kit*, International Institute for Sustainable Development, 1994, p. 102.

19. Conversation with Lewis Barton, February 26, 1997.

20. "Business Partnership Packages Services to Create Closed Loop Recycling Program," Ethan Allen press release, April 4, 1993, pp. 2–4.

21. Forcini, Hallie, "Ethan Allen Makes, Saves Money," *Green Packaging 2000*, November 1993, p. 4.

9

Work from the Inside Out

The backlash to marketers' questionable green-marketing activities of the early 1990s taught us a valuable lesson: consumers' environmental concerns cannot be exploited by merely communicating superficial product tweaks and regulatory-driven corporate responses. In other words, it is not enough to talk green; companies must *be* green. Environmental issues represent a question of survival for millions of people around the world; as Mobil and other companies learned the hard way, retaliation from consumers, environmentalists, regulators, and the media against those companies they feel are exploiting the environment can be serious, swift, and enduring.

In the words of Roy Spence, president of Austin-based GSD&M advertising, "What you stand for is just as important as what you sell." To successfully develop and market environmentally sound products and services, it is necessary to adopt a thorough approach to greening that reaches deep into corporate culture. Start with the CEO and don't stop until the pencils at corporate headquarters are "green." Many companies across the nation and around the world have already begun to substantially green their operations, bring their employees on board, and communicate their initiatives. They are finding that such greening helps them create exciting new products while helping them save money, recruit productively, and keep shareholders happy.

Following are the hallmarks and strategies of the companies in the vanguard of corporate greening. As such, they are best able to take advantage of the many opportunities of environmental consumerism.

INTEGRITY

Understand the key environmental issues facing your business and address them with *integrity*; to give only lip service is to invite scrutiny by government, environmentalists, and the media, as well as rejection by consumers quick to spot companies with insincere or incomplete environmental programs.

Conduct a thorough environmental audit to assess current performance and establish a benchmark upon which to measure progress. This will ensure that your company is in compliance with key environmental regulations, and has a topflight environmental management system in place. Shoot for compliance with ISO 14001, the management-auditing component of the newly emerging ISO 14000 series of voluntary international environmental quality standards described in Chapter 1. To build credibility and win the public's confidence, have your audits certified by an independent third party or voluntarily report your results to the EPA and the public.

PRO-ACTIVE

Go beyond what is expected by regulators and other stakeholders. Pro-actively commit to solving emerging environmental problems like ozone layer depletion or protection of rain forests. S. C. Johnson, for example, eliminated chlorofluorocarbon propellants in its aerosol products a year ahead of government mandate, and was the first company in its industry to do so. York International leapfrogged competition by being the first in its industry to use an alternative refrigerant in air-conditioner chillers.[1]

Being pro-active projects leadership, and sends a message to investors that the company is in good hands. Because regulators are less likely to impose restrictions on companies whose actions transcend minimum standards, it allows companies to help define the standards by which they will be judged. A pro-active stance also affords the greatest opportunities to find cost-effective solutions to environmental ills and beat competitors in meeting regulations and consumer expectations. Southern California Edison, for example, has already pledged a 20 percent reduction in carbon dioxide emissions by 2010.

Finally, pro-active companies are better prepared to withstand the scrutiny that overtly "green" companies often face. For instance in 1994, a controversial report in *Business Ethics* magazine put into question The Body Shop's pioneering socially and environmentally conscious practices. While the retail cosmetic chain's stock price plummeted, there is very little evidence that The Body Shop's clientele switched their purchasing habits as a result of the criticism. It is hypothesized that customers may have perceived the company's environmental performance to be so high that they were willing to discount new facts that were emerging.[2]

A VISIBLE AND COMMITTED CEO

With consumers scrutinizing products at every phase of the life cycle, environmentally pro-active companies recognize that corporate greening must extend to every department—including manufacturing, marketing, research and development, and consumer and public affairs. Only a committed chief executive with a clear vision for his or her company can add the necessary weight to the message for all employees and other environmental stakeholders to realize that environmental soundness is indeed a priority.

The need to start with the chief executive officer cannot be overemphasized. The consumer backlash against Exxon over the 1989 oil spill in Alaska's Prince William Sound may have been caused as much by CEO Lawrence Rawls's delayed appearance on the scene as it was by outrage over the environmental degradation that resulted.

In the age of environmental consumerism, chief executive officers of such leading-edge companies as Ben & Jerry's, Patagonia, Tom's of Maine, and Interface win their consumers' trust by projecting a *personal* commitment to the environment. These executives help to forge an emotional link between the company and its customers, acting as a symbolic police officer who watches over corporate operations and ensures environmental compliance. Such CEOs are especially believable because they are perceived as having a personal stake in the outcome.

EMPOWERED EMPLOYEES

CEOs, of course, are only as effective as their employees. For it is only when employees are aware of the issues and given the authority to make changes that greener products will be developed and environmentally sound practices be put in place. Use innovative and thought-provoking education and incentive programs to empower employees to develop ecologically sound processes and products. For example, many companies now expose their employees to outside speakers who talk about trends in demographics, technology, the economy, and the environment.

At Coca-Cola, all employees participate in an Environmental Development Program that discusses many of the myths and realities of environmental issues and outlines Coca-Cola's accomplishments. Ted Turner distributes copies of Lester Brown's *State of the World* to all new producers and reporters, while Texaco employees engage in an electronic environmental-education program. Scores on a follow-up quiz help to determine year-end bonuses.

Consider an innovative approach to training pioneered in Sweden with remarkable results. Called "The Natural Step," the program teaches employees to use the key principles of sustainability as a guide in making their day-to-day activities more ecologically attuned.

 Case Study

Introducing The Natural Step: An Innovative Approach to Sustainability Training

In 1989, while working to cure leukemia in children, Dr. Karl-Henrick Robert concluded the best way to prevent many cancers from occurring in the first place is by cutting down on factors in the environment linked to the disease. Together with a group of leading scientists, environmental activists, economists, and politicians, Dr. Robert established the four "system conditions" essential for sustainable living that underlie The Natural Step (TNS) Training Program he developed.

The four system conditions are:

1. Materials from Earth's crust must not be allowed to systematically increase in nature.

2. Persistent substances produced by society must not systematically increase in nature.

3. The physical basis for Earth's productive, natural cycles and biological diversity must not be systematically deteriorated.

4. There must be fair and efficient use of resources with respect to meeting human needs.

Armed with these fundamental principles, and coupled with the belief that "every successful society educates its children early and its adults continually about what is critical to survival," proponents of The Natural Step now teach environmentally safe behaviors to people in several countries around the globe, including

Canada, Britain, New Zealand, Poland, and the United States.

With the backing of King Carl Gustaf XVI, The Natural Step has distributed informational pamphlets to every school and household in Sweden, and has won the support of over 25 percent of all Swedish companies including IKEA, Electrolux, and McDonald's Sweden, who are using the program to transform their businesses.

IKEA, which began using the program in 1991, provides basic environmental training not only to all its employees but also to its suppliers. Each division applies TNS principles to its own needs. As a result, only certified tropical hardwoods from sustainable sources are allowed in IKEA products, and designers have come up with new products such as a couch with a hidden worm-composting box inside.

At Electrolux, truly CFC-free refrigerators and freezers as well as reduced costs and increased sales come from the incorporation of TNS principles into corporate policy. Electrolux now reduces carbon emissions by shipping 75 percent of its products in Europe by rail instead of by truck. As a result of TNS and a high level of awareness among consumers, Swedish paper companies have switched to almost entirely chlorine-free paper.

Noted author, environmentalist, and businessman Paul Hawken heads up the U.S. branch of TNS, founded in 1995. With a lofty goal of training 100 Fortune 1000 companies and one million people within five years, it focuses on creating a defined training system that can be licensed to various organizations, from businesses to municipalities.[3]

"GREENING" IS A CONTINUOUS PROCESS

Environmental marketing has been described as a race without a finish line. Because definitive answers to the questions of green are not always available and absolute environmental excellence is more an ideal than a realistic goal, it's best to view corporate environmentalism as a series of small steps on a learning curve. Take an inventory of emissions and by-products, develop a plan, set measurable goals, and work toward them. Constantly integrate, learn, and refine your products and processes. To help integrate environmental programs into corporate culture, consider incorporating efforts into ongoing Total Quality Management Programs.[4]

 **Case Study   One CEO's Environmental Odyssey**

According to Ray Anderson, CEO of Atlanta-based Interface, Inc., a leading maker of commercial carpet, carpet tile, and other interior furnishings, responsible management of Earth's resources is a question of business survival. In Anderson's words, "Sustainability is the key to achieving the resource efficiency that will be necessary for manufacturing companies such as ours that hope to survive, much less flourish, in the 21st century." Setting his 24-year-old, $1-billion company on course "to become the first name in commercial and industrial ecology worldwide," Anderson is encouraging Interface, with products sold in more than 110 countries, to incorporate environmentalism into every corner of the firm. Despite a product line based heavily on petrochemicals, Anderson is determined to make his company the paradigm of sustainability and zero waste. He believes that Interface's own impact can be magnified by influencing others, so Interface's example has infinite potential to make the world a better place to live.

Interface's first step toward sustainability begins with the implementation of a three-part educational program. The first is the adoption of environmental training for the entire workforce, to include training in the principles of The Natural Step for all 5,000 employees worldwide. The second is an internal "EcoSense" program which outlines a seven-front approach to sustainability and focuses on resource depletion, landfill use, pollution, and energy waste. The third part aims to increase employees' overall environmental awareness at home as well as in the workplace. By extending positive environmental steps beyond the office walls, Interface hopes to affect attitudes and extend the impact of the internal environmental program—QUEST (Quality Utilizing Employee Suggestions and Teamwork).

At Interface, education translates into profitable innovation. As of 1995, the company entered a revolutionary new phase, and raised the environmental bar in the process—they began leasing carpets through a unique Evergreen Lease Program. Under the program, Interface actually retains ownership of its carpet tile, making itself, the manufacturer, responsible for the maintenance, repair, and ultimate recycling of the carpet tile. By assuming full life cycle responsibility for its products, Interface not only ensures that the recycling loop will be closed, but also maximizes the potential to reuse natural resources while preventing a voluminous and potentially hazardous source of waste from going into landfills. The Evergreen Lease is especially effective with carpet tile because only worn tiles are replaced, thus eliminating the need to install a whole new carpet, but providing a rolling, progressive face-lift that goes on theoretically as long as the building stands.

If Interface has its way, one day its carpeting may be not just recyclable but biodegradable as well. In 1995, the R&D division developed a fully compostable carpet made of natural and degradable fibers, now undergoing testing. Meanwhile, the company continues to explore other initiatives and technologies brought about by heightened awareness internally for responsible and profitable management of environmental issues.

Interface may be in the earliest stages of its journey toward becoming a sustainable company, but it is already profiting significantly in the process. Through QUEST, part of the company's overall environmental initiative, Interface has saved more than $20 million. Thanks to QUEST, the company now produces 100 percent post-industrial recycled nylon carpet, enjoys a 25 percent improved efficiency of turnover for beams of yarn, a 16 percent reduction in hexane solvent usage with the implementation of a new carpet-drying procedure, and a 75 percent reduction in scrap yarn from beams at one of their manufacturing sites. In addition, Interface has retrofitted machinery that consumes less energy, and steam water used for dyeing is starting to be recaptured.

These, along with many other efforts, have boosted efficiency and waste reduction while lowering operating costs and thus increasing profits. The company encourages employees to identify new ways in which the company can achieve its 1997 goal of reducing their waste by 50 percent relative to the amount produced in 1994. By the company's own calculations, this represents a possible savings of approximately $35 million.[5]

COMMUNICATION

When it comes to environmental performance, it is not enough for a company to simply assert a strong commitment to environmental cleanup and preservation. The company must be publicly accountable and viewed as continuously improving its environmental performance.

Regularly report on progress by issuing annual environmental reports and field special advertising and public relations efforts. In addition to environment-related messages, companies such as Ben & Jerry's Homemade, Inc., of Waterbury, Vermont, go so far as to issue annual social audits of their firm's community-oriented activities.

Contrary to what many in industry may think, public disclosure of information is not to be feared as a competitive disadvantage or an invitation to litigation. Its benefits outweigh the risks. As noted by Art Kleiner writing in the *Harvard Business Review*:

The "Emergency Planning and Right to Know Provision" (Title III) of the Superfund Amendments and Reauthorization Act that since 1986 has required companies to report their emission levels of 300 hazardous chemicals, has resulted in very few citizen group protests or even requests for more information. People chiefly want to be kept informed. The public will accept reasonable progress.[6]

Openness is a key factor in building credibility and quelling consumer concern about the adverse environmental impacts of a firm's activities. As interest in *Shopping for a Better World* suggests, consumers want to know who they are buying from. The guidebook helps to demystify the manufacturers behind the products, providing consumers with a peek inside. So, establish credibility and build relationships with consumers by opening the doors—conduct plant tours, disclose information honestly and clearly, and run special environmental hotlines.

In Germany, chemical manufacturers recognize that the mysterious nature of their manufacturing plants creates suspicion among community residents. To help overcome the fear that results, manufacturers embarked on a campaign of openness, conducting plant tours for local residents and interested parties. In the United States and Canada, chemical manufacturers such as Dow Chemical and Polaroid utilize similar openness strategies as part of Responsible Care, an industry-wide program. Seeking to reestablish credibility and bring the industry's image more in line with consumer expectations, the Responsible Care program sets out a code of standards and practices in the areas of health, safety, and the environment, and requires member companies to establish objectives, develop strategies and action plans, and monitor and report progress to the public—good or bad.

Communications can help to counter a negative environmental image and address consumer skepticism head on. Once on the blacklist of eco-warriors, McDonald's reversed its negative image by communicating a number of substantive initiatives including internal, behind-the-counter greening and other activities visible to restaurant patrons as well as other stakeholders. Big pronouncements like "We're willing to buy $100,000,000 in recycled products this year," and "We use the most recycled paper," supported by bold moves like the switch from polystyrene clamshells to source-reduced quilt-wraps and use of recycled furniture has catapulted McDonald's to the top of consumers' lists of environmentally reputable companies.[7]

Notes

1. "The Hole Truth," *The Green Business Letter*, Makower, Joel, ed., January 1996, p. 8.
2. Miller, Joyce, and Francisco Szekely, "Becoming Green: Can Companies Do It Cost Effectively?" *Corporate Environmental Strategy*, Volume 3, Number 2, December 1995, p. 63.
3. Scott, Mary, "Will It Be a Natural Step Here?" *Business Ethics*, January/February 1996, p. 18; Banks, Jim, ed., "The Natural Step for Designers," *Green Design*, Volume 2, Number 3, Spring 1996, p. 3; Eronn, Robert, Swedish Institute, "The Natural Step—a Social Invention for the Environment," Number 401, December 1993, p. 7.
4. A good resource for companies intending to integrate environmental programs into Total Quality Management Programs is the Global Environment Management Initiative located in Washington, D.C. Founded for the purpose of helping business assert leadership in the area of environmental management, it has helped to spearhead the practice of Total Quality Environmental Management, along with a journal of the same name. Members include Eastman Kodak, Colgate-Palmolive, AT&T, DuPont, Weyerhaeuser, and others.

5. Personal communication with Lisa Cape, February 14, 1997.
6. Kleiner, Art, "What Does it Mean to Be Green?" *Harvard Business Review*, July–August 1991, p. 42.
7. Stisser, Peter, "A Deeper Shade of Green," *American Demographics*, March 1994, p. 28.

10

Two Companies That Do Everything Right

The strategies for reaping the opportunities of environmental consumerism are numerous and far reaching. They not only represent a shift in communications strategy, but a thorough approach to product development together with the ability to forge constructive coalitions with a wide array of corporate environmental stakeholders. Taken together, these strategies reinforce each other to shape a complete and credible response to consumers' environmental concerns. Using them in concert provides marketers with the best chance to reap the many rewards of being green.

There is much to learn from companies who are pioneering these strategies and enjoying the benefits. It is these companies and their strategies that we turn to in this chapter. While many companies both large and small fit into this category—two have been chosen to be profiled in depth: Tom's of Maine and Patagonia.

Consumer loyalty to these companies and their offerings proves that environmental strategies can form the basis of an enduring business and provide leverage in the face of formidable competition. They superbly demonstrate how green marketing strategies can create jobs, build insurmountable brand loyalties, and return hefty profits while contributing to an environmentally sustainable society.

 Case Study

Tom's of Maine: Where Corporate Social Responsibility Is a Way of Life

In 1970, the husband-and-wife team of Tom and Kate Chappell co-founded their Kennebunk, Maine, natural personal-care products firm with a mission: to create products that were more healthful to use, and to produce those products in synergy with their community and environment. One of the most successful small corporations in America today, Tom's of Maine is living proof that it is in fact possible to integrate personal values with managing for all traditional goals of business—making money, expanding market share, increasing profits, and building customer loyalty.

The makers of the fast-growing Tom's of Maine line of toothpaste, deodorant, soap, and mouthwash founded their company on the notion that humans, animals, and all other forms of nature deserve dignity and respect. Their commitment to social responsibility is not taken lightly. According to Nancy Rosenzweig, the firm's director of corporate communications, "You have to be intentional about walking your talk. It influences every aspect of the way we do business, from how we listen to and respond to our consumers, how we treat our employees (flexible work schedules and job sharing are commonplace), to how we interact with the community, how we deal with our trading partners, how we deal with the environment, and, ultimately, how we share our profits." It is also never-ending. Adds Rosenzweig, "You may never achieve perfection but you must always be working toward narrowing the gap between your mission and your actions."

A Thorough Approach to Product Development

Accordingly, the firm makes its products with the highest quality natural ingredients without additives, preservatives, artificial flavors, or fragrances. Packaging is also responsible. Tom's of Maine toothpaste, for example, comes in a recyclable aluminum tube inserted in a box made from 100 percent recycled cardboard and printed with soy-based inks.

Unique in the marketing world, Tom's of Maine lists all ingredients on product labels together with the specific purpose and source of each ingredient. Regis Park, assistant manager of communications, tells why the company provides so much detailed information: "We share more up-front information with consumers than anyone else. We assume they are intelligent and discriminating, and that they want to make informed choices."

To reinforce its commitment to consumers, Tom and Kate Chappell's signatures appear on every product label and the company answers each consumer letter personally. Says Rosenzweig, "When you have a dialogue between two real people, there is a

---

Exhibit 10.1
Tom's of Maine Ingredient Statement

How do we define *natural* ? By *natural* we mean that the product contains no artificial preservatives, artificial dyes, or artificial sweeteners (like saccharin) and is created with minimally processed ingredients originally sourced in nature. On each box we list our ingredients, their purpose and source. We believe you have a right to know. Ⓤ

Active Ingredient	Purpose	Source
Sodium monofluorophosphate	Decay prevention	Fluorspar (calcium fluoride), an ore
Ingredient		
Calcium carbonate	Mild abrasive	Purified calcium from the earth
Glycerin	Moistener	By-product of vegetable oil soap (Kosher)
Water	Consistency	Branch Brook
Sodium lauryl sulfate	Disperse the calcium	Derived from coconut oil
Carrageenan	Thickener	Seaweed
Cinnamon & peppermint oils with other natural flavors	Flavor	Cinnamon & peppermint plants

NO SACCHARIN ✳ NO ARTIFICIAL SWEETENERS OR PRESERVATIVES ✳ NO ARTIFICIAL COLOR OR FLAVOR
NO ANIMAL INGREDIENTS

© Copyright 1997 Tom's of Maine, Inc.

Source: Used with permission of Tom's of Maine

heightened sense of understanding and responsibility. Just as in a personal friendship, when we don't do something right, we say we're sorry and work to correct it."

Family and Community Orientation

The parents of five children themselves, Tom and Kate Chappell demonstrate a strong commitment to family-oriented policies. Tom's of Maine offers its employees a one-month maternity or paternity leave, partial child-care reimbursement for employees earning less than $32,000 annually, flexible work schedules, and a child-care referral service. Acknowledging the business benefits of such policies, Tom Chappell notes, "Show your employees respect and concern, demonstrate that you care about the quality of their lives, and you'll get loyalty and hard work in return." These family-friendly policies have earned Tom's of Maine a coveted spot on *Working Mother* magazine's annual list of 100 Best Companies for Working Parents.

The company takes its responsibility to the community seriously as well, donating 10 percent of pre-tax profits to charitable causes. This represents one of the highest percentage donations of any corporation in America. Much of that money supports environmental concerns such as recycling and conservation. In 1991, with financial support and the loan-out of an employee affectionately known as "The Trash Lady," the company helped the town of Kennebunk start its first recycling program. It is now engaged in a 15-year relationship with Community Partners, Inc., a facility for the mentally and physically challenged, providing job opportunities for several of the group's clients. In addition, employees can donate 5 percent of their paid work time to participation in community service activities. Regis Park ends each day by calling an elderly shut-in man in Wells, Maine, as part of a Tender Loving Callers program in her community.

Competitive Advantage

At Tom's of Maine, a little respect for the consumer and a policy of openness is paying off. Their offerings command a 20 to 50 percent premium, depending on the product and market, and in 1995, the company's sales were $20 million, up over 25 percent since 1991.

Moreover, what started as a profitable niche opportunity is now finding its way into the mainstream. The full line of Tom's of Maine brand natural personal-care products is now distributed in 7,000 health-food stores throughout the United States, Canada, and England, as well as 20,000 food and drug outlets on the east and west coasts.

Admittedly, Tom's of Maine's environmental and social strategies are not based purely on altruism. Rosenzweig concedes, "The environmental and social responsibility policies are a barrier to competitive advances. Even a competitor with much greater resources cannot just replicate our formula and expect to take our market share. Our corporate practices add a richness and depth to our product appeal that creates an unusually strong brand loyalty." Indeed, Patti Murphy, Consumer Relations Coordinator, reports that the company receives more than 75 letters a week from consumers. She notes the one theme that dominates the consumer mail is an appreciation for Tom's of Maine's values.

Tom's of Maine's pioneering policies, which are detailed at greater length in Tom Chappell's book, *Soul of a Business*, have not gone unnoticed by other corporate environmental stakeholders. In 1992, the company received the prestigious Corporate Conscience Award for Charitable Contributions from the Council on Economic Priorities. In 1993, the Chappells were presented with the New England Environmental Leadership Award and the Governor's Award for Business Excellence.

Case Study

Patagonia: A Deep-Seated Commitment to Environmentalism

At Patagonia, Inc., headquartered in Ventura, California, catering to Alpine and other outdoor enthusiasts means much more than just designing and selling the highest-quality outerwear. It means making a deep commitment to pressing environmental and social concerns as well. By developing an environmentally conscious corporate culture and supporting the environmental causes and groups its customers care most about, Patagonia has hit upon a winning business formula that sets it apart from all other outerwear marketers, and stands as a shining example for all environmentally minded businesses. Their "doing well by doing good" strategy is paying off in stellar sales and fiercely loyal customers.

Patagonia's reputation for innovative social and environmental responsibility extends back to the company's roots. Founder Yvon Chouinard started Patagonia in the late 1960s as a sister to the Chouinard Equipment Company, purveyors of hardware for Alpine climbing and other outdoor activities. When Chouinard realized that climbing equipment adversely affected the pristine wilderness setting in which it was used, he decided to make his equipment environmentally responsible, offering an innovative alternative to the bolts that were traditionally used.

Although Chouinard Equipment Company has since been sold, the environmentally responsible tradition lives on at Patagonia. The company takes environmental issues into consideration in all aspects of its business, from the materials in its clothing and the construction details in its retail stores to supporting various environmental causes of concern to its customers.

Edible Landscaping

Patagonia's commitment starts with an internal assessment that helps the company understand and prioritize opportunities to minimize environmental impact. Everything from the wood and lighting in Patagonia's retail stores to the food in the corporate cafeteria has been scrutinized for possible environmental harm. The company now maintains an extensive recycling program, composts its food waste, uses low-flow toilets, and participates in the U.S. Environmental Protection Agency's voluntary Green Lights energy-efficient lighting program. Even the grounds around company headquarters feature edible landscaping—banana trees.

Outerwear with Minimal Environmental Impact

Patagonia works closely with suppliers to minimize the environmental impact of its clothes. In 1993, Patagonia was one of the first customers for Wellman's EcoSpun fiber, which they incorporated into fleece jackets and pants redubbed Synchilla PCR (for post-consumer recycled). Anxious to help build the market for this innovative material, Patagonia spread the word on "PCR Synchilla" within the industry and, today, the use of recycled materials in various types of fabrics is widespread, helping to keep costs low for all.

To help cut down on the pollution of soil, air, and water associated with cotton farming, which is chemically intensive despite its benign image, Patagonia uses only organically grown cotton, effective with the spring 1996 line. To avoid letting the relative expense of organic cotton stand in its way, Patagonia chose to "split the difference" with consumers, reducing its margin while asking them to accept a $2–$10 price increase on each garment. To help enlist their support for the more sustainable alternative, Patagonia educated their consumers about the environmental imperative of growing cotton organically. Educational efforts included extensive customer communications including an essay in the Spring 1996 catalog by Yvon Chouinard, and an interactive display in its Ventura headquarters (see Chapter 6).

As part of its attempts to reduce the environmental impact of its products, Patagonia simply makes fewer of them. Supporting the company's corporate goal to be a model sustainable enterprise, in 1993, the company decided to limit its product line to 280 styles. In Chouinard's words, this decision stems from the desire "to avoid cluttering the world with a lot of things people can't use." High-quality, durable products don't have to be replaced often, and when outgrown can be passed along for further use. He dubs the idea of capping the size of the company "Natural Growth," because it mimics a principle of nature—if something gets too big for the community, it will die. Likewise, if the size of the company gets out of control, it can outgrow its consumer support.

Support for Environmental Groups and Causes

Patagonia reinforces its strong ties to consumers by supporting the environmental groups and causes they care most about. Each year, Patagonia pledges 1 percent of its sales or 10 percent of pre-tax profits, whichever is greater, to groups actively working in such areas as biodiversity, old-growth forests, environmentally preferable methods of resource extraction, alternative energy, water, social activism, and environmental education. Referring to this commitment as an "Earth Tax," Patagonia donates primarily to the smaller environmental groups and organizations working on local environmental protection initiatives which may have difficulty receiving funds from other sources. As an example, Patagonia supported the "Friends of the Ventura River" group to clean up an unofficial bird sanctuary bordering the Ventura River near the corporate head-quarters. Among its commitments, Patagonia is a founding member of the Conservation Alliance, an organization of like-minded companies seeking to give back to the outdoors.

Contrary to the more conservative sentiments of many a mass marketer, Patagonia is not afraid to support controversial groups and causes such as Planned Parenthood (the company views population growth as a critical environmental problem), or the now-defunct Earth First! group. While acknowledging that such efforts will offend some would-be customers, Patagonia believes its most loyal patrons support the same causes, or will at least respect the company for taking a stand.

Through April 1997, Patagonia contributed more than $8 million to hundreds of organizations including the Access Fund, the Surfrider Foundation, and the Earth Conservation Corps.

Communicating with Customers

Patagonia communicates environmental messages to its consumers through essays in its seasonal catalogs, in-store communiqués, and paid advertising. Ads placed in select outdoor-oriented magazines inform customers of product developments as well as emerging environmental issues and Patagonia's activities. In addition, the company publishes an annual "Green Report" detailing progress against all key environment-related goals.

Business Success—Public Recognition

Patagonia's commitment to quality and its pioneering environmental and social practices add up to more than just business success. In little more than a decade, Patagonia has amassed $150 million in annual sales throughout the United States, Japan, and Europe. In addition, the company has won numerous awards, including the American Marketing Association's 1995 special Edison Award for Corporate Environmental Achievement, a listing in *The Nation*'s Top 100 Companies, and a nine-year stint on *Working Mother* magazine's 100 Best Companies for Working Parents. Yvon Chouinard was also invited to participate in a Corporate Responsibility Roundtable held at the White House in 1996.

While sales and accolades are important at Patagonia, it is clear the company manages with an eye on a double bottom line, measured by a strong corporate culture and recognition as a force for social and environmental change. Their success provides a lesson to other businesses looking to garner profits while furthering environmental and social priorities.

Conclusion

Successful green marketing entails much more than simply tweaking the size of a package, using recycled materials in place of virgin ones, or substituting natural ingredients for synthetic. While positive and necessary, such changes are just a small part of a much, much bigger picture. Look at those businesses at the forefront of the green trend and see a deeper characteristic than just greened-up products or ads that make them at once environmental and societal leaders as well as profitable: green leaders are driven by more than short-term financial goals. They are motivated by a double bottom line, a bottom line that recognizes the potential for business to effect societal change as well as create economic wealth. A business that at the end of the day is measured by its contribution to human potential and the harmony of its objectives with other living beings as much as by its profits.

Green leaders are not afraid to project the values that underlie their organization's mission and purpose. To their customers, the products they sell are not just consumables sold at a profit but mirrors of their corporate commitment to environmental care and social responsibility. Such products appeal to consumers with a finely honed sense of idealism, integrity, and the belief that businesses can and should achieve social goals as well as financial ones.

Because green leaders are not afraid to take a stand on their beliefs, their consumers stand ready to believe their product claims and regard the individuals running the company as sincere.

The most successful green companies operate holistically. Unlike conventional marketers who generally react to consumers' immediate needs, the most successful green companies lead their customers and other stakeholders, rather than accept being led by them. They anticipate emerging environmental issues and address them before being forced to do so. They are then able to set their own agenda with regulators and they don't risk disappointing their customers or shaking their confidence.

Rather than simply employ resources at hand, the deep-seated convictions of the founders and CEOs of the most environmentally responsible companies challenge their employees to stretch beyond their immediate horizons, teaming up with corporate environmental stakeholders to create optimal solutions to pressing environmental problems.

These leaders are not afraid to question assumptions or break the rules. They derive competitive advantage while accomplishing the most good for society by embracing unconventional and often radical solutions. They enhance profitability and quality by innovating more and more efficient ways to design and market products and conduct their businesses overall.

The greenest companies are not afraid to listen—to understand the issues from all sides, to pick up clues from individuals and groups on the fringes who can lead them to new opportunities, and to simply demonstrate to employees, customers, suppliers, and others that they care. At the same time, they are not afraid to trust. They are open to entrees from government regulators offering technical assistance or to an environmentalist with a seemingly offbeat idea. Most important, they trust their instincts, their insights into the causes of and probable solutions to society's environmental ills, and their own deeply held beliefs.

Green leaders focus—on the stakeholders most important to

their business and on the product attributes that represent the greatest environmental impact and are most important to their customers.

Finally, green leaders are patient. They are committed to the long term, and to continuous improvement. They are eager to learn from their own mistakes and they engage in forums that allow them to learn from the mistakes of others. And, like Sally Fox, who took 10 years to cultivate a naturally colored cotton seed capable of yielding a fiber long enough to be spun into marketable yarn, green leaders persevere.

A green future is now being created by visionaries with a competitive spirit in their bellies and social activism in their hearts. While many businesspeople may still be content to tweak products or manage cash cows in the quest for next quarter's earnings, green leaders are right now readying new products and services to market, creating new industries and more inclusive work and management styles that didn't exist five or ten years ago. Theirs will be the standards for the future.

With ever-increasing scientific understanding of how Earth works, a general movement toward safer, less polluting, and more environmentally sustainable practices is inevitable. Marketers who take the time now to court the deepest-green consumers with truly innovative solutions to environmental concerns will be the ones who reap the biggest future opportunities.

The CERES Principles *

INTRODUCTION

By adopting these Principles, we publicly affirm our belief that corporations have a responsibility for the environment, and must conduct all aspects of their business as responsible stewards of the environment by operating in a manner that protects the Earth. We believe that corporations must not compromise the ability of future generations to sustain themselves.

We will update our practices constantly in light of advances in technology and new understandings in health and environmental science. In collaboration with CERES, we will promote a dynamic process to ensure that the Principles are interpreted in a way that accommodates changing technologies and environmental realities. We intend to make consistent, measurable progress in imple-

*Used with permission of Coalition for Environmentally Responsible Economies

menting these Principles and to apply them to all aspects of our operations throughout the world.

Protection of the Biosphere

We will reduce and make continual progress toward eliminating the release of any substance that may cause environmental damage to the air, water, or the earth or its inhabitants. We will safeguard all habitats affected by our operations and will protect open spaces and wilderness, while preserving biodiversity.

Sustainable Use of Natural Resources

We will make sustainable use of renewable natural resources, such as water, soils and forests. We will conserve nonrenewable natural resources through efficient use and careful planning.

Reduction and Disposal of Wastes

We will reduce and where possible eliminate waste through source reduction and recycling. All waste will be handled and disposed of through safe and responsible methods.

Energy Conservation

We will conserve energy and improve the energy efficiency of our internal operations and of the goods and services we sell. We will make every effort to use environmentally safe and sustainable energy sources.

Risk Reduction

We will strive to minimize the environmental, health and safety risks to our employees and the communities in which we operate through safe technologies, facilities and operating procedures, and by being prepared for emergencies.

Safe Products and Services

We will reduce and where possible eliminate the use, manufacture or sale of products and services that cause environmental damage or health or safety hazards. We will inform our customers of the environmental impacts of our products or services and try to correct unsafe use.

Environmental Restoration

We will promptly and responsibly correct conditions we have caused that endanger health, safety or the environment. To the extent feasible, we will redress injuries we have caused to persons or damage we have caused to the environment and will restore the environment.

Informing the Public

We will inform in a timely manner everyone who may be affected by conditions caused by our company that might endanger health, safety or the environment. We will regularly seek advice and counsel through dialogue with persons in communities near our facilities. We will not take any action against employees for reporting dangerous incidents or conditions to management or to appropriate authorities.

Management Commitment

We will implement these Principles and sustain a process that ensures that the Board of Directors and Chief Executive Officer are fully informed about pertinent environmental issues and are fully responsible for environmental policy. In selecting our Board of Directors, we will consider demonstrated environmental commitment as a factor.

Audits and Reports

We will conduct an annual self-evaluation of our progress in implementing these Principles. We will support the timely creation of generally accepted environmental audit procedures. We will annually complete the CERES Report, which will be made available to the public.

DISCLAIMER

These Principles establish an environmental ethic with criteria by which investors and others can assess the environmental performance of companies. Companies that endorse these Principles pledge to go voluntarily beyond the requirements of the law. The terms may and might in Principles one and eight are not meant to encompass every imaginable consequence, no matter how remote. Rather, these Principles obligate endorsers to behave as prudent persons who are not governed by conflicting interests and who possess a strong commitment to environmental excellence and to human health and safety. These Principles are not intended to create new legal liabilities, expand existing rights or obligations, waive legal defenses, or otherwise affect the legal position of any endorsing company, and are not intended to be used against an endorser in any legal proceeding for any purpose.

CERES PRINCIPLES ENDORSING COMPANIES

Dozens of companies have endorsed the CERES Principles. They represent a range of sizes, from the tiny entrepreneurial to the Fortune 500; geographic locations, from local to worldwide operations; and products and services, from foods to lumber to medical products to financial services. They all share a commitment on the highest level to ecologically sound operations and public environmental reporting.

- Arizona Public Service Company

- Aurora Press

- Aveda Corporation

- Bellcomb Technologies, Inc.

- Ben & Jerry's Homemade

- Bestmann Green Systems, Inc.
- Bethlehem Steel Corporation
- The Body Shop International
- The Bullitt Foundation
- Calvert Social Investment Fund
- Co-op America
- Council on Economic Priorities
- Earth Communications, Inc.
- Earth Friendly Products, Inc.
- Earthrise Trading Company
- Eco-Invest Publishing, Ltd.
- Ecoprint
- Environmental Risk & Loss Control, Inc.
- First Affirmative Financial Network
- Franklin Research & Development Corporation
- General Motors Corporation
- Global Environmental Technologies
- GreenAudit
- Harrington Investments
- Harwood Products Company
- H. B. Fuller Company
- LecTec Corporation
- Louisville & Jefferson Metropolitan Sewer District

- Membran Corporation

- Nature's Fresh Northwest

- New Heights Schools

- NewLeaf Designs, Inc.

- Polaroid Corporation

- Progressive Asset Management

- Real Goods Trading Corporation

- Recycled Paper Company

- Stonyfield Farm Yogurt

- Sullivan & Worcester

- The Summit Group

- Sun Company, Inc.

- Target Energy

- The Timberland Company

- Tom's of Maine

- Town Creek Industries

- Tree-Free EcoPaper

- United States Trust Company of Boston

- VanCity Savings Credit Union

- Walnut Acres

- The WATER Foundation

- County of Westchester, New York

Federal Trade Commission Guides for the Use of Environmental Marketing Claims

On October 4, 1996, The Federal Trade Commission announced a new and improved version of its Environmental Marketing Guidelines. The updated guidelines reflect changing consumer perceptions about what various environmental claims mean and the emergence of new claims since these FTC guides first were announced in July 1992. Additional guidance is now provided on the use of environmental seal-of-approval logos and the chasing-arrows symbol, as well as for such marketing claims as "environmentally preferable," "non-toxic," and "chlorine free." The guidelines retain the section on general advertising principles and continue to address specific categories of environmental benefit claims, such as degradable, recycled content, and ozone friendly.

Minor changes also have been made in a few instances for purposes of clarification.

Important note: The Commission is currently reviewing the Compostable and Recyclable sections of the Guides, § 260.7 (c)-(d). These sections remain in effect during the review process. The Commission is also considering whether product parts that can be reconditioned and/or reused in the manufacture of new products can be claimed to be "recyclable" under the Guides, and whether products manufactured from such reconditioned and/or reused parts can be labeled "recycled" under the Guides. For further information, please call 202-326-3022.

The revised guidelines are effective immediately, and the 1992 guidelines on recyclable and compostable claims continue to remain in effect unless subsequently amended.

The following are the revised guidelines:

Part 260 sec.
260.1 Statement of Purpose.
260.2 Scope of guides.
260.3 Structure of the guides.
260.4 Review procedure.
260.5 Interpretation and substantiation of environmental marketing claims.
260.6 General principles.
260.7 Environmental marketing claims.
260.8 Environmental assessment.

Authority: 15 U.S.C. §§ 41–58

260.1 Statement of purpose

These guides represent administrative interpretations of laws administered by the Federal Trade Commission for the guidance of the public in conducting its affairs in conformity with legal requirements. These guides specifically address the application of Section 5 of the FTC Act to environmental advertising and marketing practices. They provide the basis for voluntary compliance with such laws by members of industry. Conduct inconsistent with the positions articulated in these guides may result in corrective action by the Commission under Section 5 if, after investigation, the Commission has reason to believe that the behavior falls within the scope of conduct declared unlawful by the statute.

260.2 Scope of guides

These guides apply to environmental claims included in labeling, advertising, promotional materials and all other forms of marketing, whether asserted directly or by implication, through words, symbols, emblems, logos, depictions, product brand names, or through any other means. The guides apply to any claim about the environmental attributes of a product or package in connection with the sale, offering for sale, or marketing of such product or package for personal, family or household use, or for commercial, institutional or industrial use.

Because the guides are not legislative rules under Section 18 of the FTC Act, they are not themselves enforceable regulations, nor do they have the force and effect of law. The guides themselves do not preempt regulation of other federal agencies or of state and local bodies governing the use of environmental marketing claims. Compliance with federal, state or local law and regulations concerning such claims, however, will not necessarily preclude Commission law enforcement action under Section 5.

260.3 Structure of the guides

The guides are composed of general principles and specific guidance on the use of environmental claims. These general principles and specific guidance are followed by examples that generally address a single deception concern. A given claim may raise issues that are addressed under more than one example and in more than one section of the guides.

In many of the examples, one or more options are presented

for qualifying a claim. These options are intended to provide a "safe harbor" for marketers who want certainty about how to make environmental claims. They do not represent the only permissible approaches to qualifying a claim. The examples do not illustrate all possible acceptable claims or disclosures that would be permissible under Section 5. In addition, some of the illustrative disclosures may be appropriate for use on labels but not in print or broadcast advertisements and vice versa. In some instances, the guides indicate within the example in what context or contexts a particular type of disclosure should be considered.

260.4 Review procedure

The Commission will review the guides as part of its general program of reviewing all industry guides on an ongoing basis. Parties may petition the Commission to alter or amend these guides in light of substantial new evidence regarding consumer interpretation of a claim or regarding substantiation of a claim. Following review of such a petition, the Commission will take such action as it deems appropriate.

260.5 Interpretation and substantiation of environmental marketing claims

Section 5 of the FTC Act makes unlawful deceptive acts and practices in or affecting commerce. The Commission's criteria for determining whether an express or implied claim has been made are enunciated in the Commission's Policy Statement on Deception.[1] In addition, any party making an express or implied claim that presents an objective assertion about the environmental attribute of a product or package must, at the time the claim is made, possess and rely upon a reasonable basis substantiating the claim. A reasonable basis consists of competent and reliable evidence. In the context of environmental marketing claims, such substantiation will often require competent and reliable scientific evidence, defined as tests, analyses, research, studies or other evidence based on the expertise of professionals in the relevant area, conducted and evaluated in an objective manner by persons qualified to do so, using procedures generally accepted in the profession to yield accurate and reliable results. Further guidance on the reasonable basis standard is set forth in the Commission's 1983 Policy Statement on the Advertising Substantiation Doctrine. 49 Fed. Reg. 30999 (1984); *appended to Thompson Medical Co.*, 104 F.T.C. 648 (1984). The Commission has also taken action in a number of cases involving alleged deceptive or unsubstantiated environmental advertising claims. A current list of environmental marketing cases and/or copies of individual cases can be obtained by calling the FTC Public Reference Branch at (202) 326-2222.

260.6 General principles

The following general principles apply to all environmental marketing claims, including, but not limited to, those described in § 260.7. In addition, § 260.7 contains specific guidance applicable to certain environmental marketing claims. Claims should comport with all relevant provisions of these guides, not simply the provision that seems most directly applicable.

(a) *Qualifications and Disclosures:* The Commission traditionally has held that in order to be effective, any qualifications or disclosures such as those described in these guides should be sufficiently clear and prominent to prevent deception. Clarity of language, relative type size and proximity to the claim being qualified, and an absence of contrary claims that could undercut effectiveness, will maximize the likelihood that the qualifications and disclosures are appropriately clear and prominent.

(b) *Distinction Between Benefits of Product and Package:* An environmental marketing claim should be presented in a way that makes clear whether the environmental attribute or benefit being asserted refers to the product, the product's packaging or to a portion or component of the product or packaging. In general, if the environmental attribute or benefit applies to all but minor, incidental components of a product or package, the claim need not be qualified to identify that fact. There may be exceptions to this general principle. For example, if an unqualified "recyclable" claim is made and the presence of the incidental component significantly limits the ability to recycle the product, then the claim would be deceptive.

Example 1: A box of aluminum foil is labeled with the claim "recyclable," without further elaboration. Unless the type of product, surrounding language, or other context of the phrase establishes whether the claim refers to the foil or the box, the claim is deceptive if any part of either the box or the foil, other than minor, incidental components, cannot be recycled.

Example 2: A soft drink bottle is labeled "recycled." The bottle is made entirely from recycled materials, but the bottle cap is not. Because reasonable consumers are likely to consider the bottle cap to be a minor, incidental component of the package, the claim is not deceptive. Similarly, it would not be deceptive to label a shopping bag "recycled" where the bag is made entirely of recycled material but the easily detachable handle, an incidental component, is not.

(c) Overstatement of Environmental Attribute: An environmental marketing claim should not be presented in a manner that overstates the environmental attribute or benefit, expressly or by implication. Marketers should avoid implications of significant environmental benefits if the benefit is in fact negligible.

Example 1: A package is labeled, "50% more recycled content than before." The manufacturer increased the recycled content of its package from 2 percent recycled material to 3 percent recycled material. Although the claim is technically true, it is likely to convey the false impression that the advertiser has increased significantly the use of recycled material.

Example 2: A trash bag is labeled "recyclable" without qualification. Because trash bags will ordinarily not be separated out from other trash at the landfill or incinerator for recycling, they are highly unlikely to be used again for any purpose. Even if the bag is technically capable of being recycled, the claim is deceptive since it asserts an environmental benefit where no significant or meaningful benefit exists.

Example 3: A paper grocery sack is labeled "reusable." The sack can be brought back to the store and reused for carrying groceries but will fall apart after two or three reuses, on average. Because reasonable consumers are unlikely to assume that a paper grocery sack is durable, the unqualified claim does not overstate the environmental benefit conveyed to consumers. The claim is not deceptive and does not need to be qualified to indicate the limited reuse of the sack.

Example 4: A package of paper coffee filters is labeled "These filters were made with a chlorine-free bleaching process." The filters are bleached with a process that releases into the environment a reduced, but still significant, amount of the same harmful byproducts associated with chlorine bleaching. The claim is likely to overstate the product's benefits because it is likely to be interpreted by consumers to mean that the product's manufacture does not cause any of the environmental risks posed by chlorine bleaching. A claim, however, that the filters were "bleached with a process that substantially reduces, but does not eliminate, harmful substances associated with chlorine bleaching" would not, if substantiated, overstate the product's benefits and is unlikely to be deceptive.

(d) Comparative Claims: Environmental marketing claims that include a comparative statement should be presented in a manner that makes the basis for the comparison sufficiently clear to avoid consumer deception. In addition, the advertiser should be able to substantiate the comparison.

Example 1: An advertiser notes that its shampoo bottle contains "20% more recycled content." The claim in its context is ambiguous. Depending on contextual factors, it could be a comparison either to the advertiser's immediately preceding product or to a competitor's product. The advertiser should clarify the claim to make the basis for comparison clear, for example, by saying "20% more recycled content than our previous package." Otherwise, the advertiser should be prepared to substantiate whatever comparison is conveyed to reasonable consumers.

Example 2: An advertiser claims that "our plastic diaper liner has the most recycled content." The advertised diaper does have more recycled content, calculated as a percentage of weight, than any other on the market, although it is still well under 100% recycled. Provided the recycled content and the comparative difference between the product and those of competitors are significant and provided the specific comparison can be substantiated, the claim is not deceptive.

Example 3: An ad claims that the advertiser's packaging creates "less waste than the leading national brand." The advertiser's source reduction was implemented sometime ago and is supported by a calculation comparing the relative solid waste contributions of the two packages. The advertiser should be able to substantiate that the comparison remains accurate.

260.7 Environmental marketing claims

Guidance about the use of environmental marketing claims is set forth below. Each guide is followed by several examples that illustrate, but do not provide an exhaustive list of, claims that do and do not comport with the guides. In each case, the general principles set forth in § 260.6 should also be followed.[2]

(a) General Environmental Benefit Claims: It is deceptive to misrepresent, directly or by implication, that a product or package offers a general environmental benefit. Unqualified general claims of environmental benefit are difficult to interpret, and depending on their context, may convey a wide range of meanings to consumers. In many cases, such claims may convey that the product or package has specific and far-reaching environmental benefits. As explained in the Commission's Ad Substantiation Statement, every express and material, implied claim that the general asser-

tion conveys to reasonable consumers about an objective quality, feature or attribute of a product must be substantiated. Unless this substantiation duty can be met, broad environmental claims should either be avoided or qualified, as necessary, to prevent deception about the specific nature of the environmental benefit being asserted.

Example 1: A brand name like "Eco-Safe" would be deceptive if, in the context of the product so named, it leads consumers to believe that the product has environmental benefits which cannot be substantiated by the manufacturer. The claim would not be deceptive if "Eco-Safe" were followed by clear and prominent qualifying language limiting the safety representation to a particular product attribute for which it could be substantiated, and provided that no other deceptive implications were created by the context.

Example 2: A product wrapper is printed with the claim "Environmentally Friendly." Textual comments on the wrapper explain that the wrapper is "Environmentally Friendly because it was not chlorine bleached, a process that has been shown to create harmful substances." The wrapper was, in fact, not bleached with chlorine. However, the production of the wrapper now creates and releases to the environment significant quantities of other harmful substances. Since consumers are likely to interpret the "Environmentally Friendly" claim, in combination with the textual explanation, to mean that no significant harmful substances are currently released to the environment, the "Environmentally Friendly" claim would be deceptive.

Example 3: A pump spray product is labeled "environmentally safe." Most of the product's active ingredients consist of volatile organic compounds (vocs) that may cause smog by contributing to ground-level ozone formation. The claim is deceptive because, absent further qualification, it is likely to convey to consumers that use of the product will not result in air pollution or other harm to the environment.

Example 4: A lawn care pesticide is advertised as "essentially non-toxic" and "practically non-toxic." Consumers would likely interpret these claims in the context of such a product as applying not only to human health effects but also to the product's environmental effects. Since the claims would likely convey to consumers that the product does not pose any risk to humans or the environment, if the pesticide in fact poses a significant risk to humans or environment, the claims would be deceptive.

Example 5: A product label contains an environmental seal, either in the form of a globe icon, or a globe icon with only the text "Earth Smart" around it. Either label is likely to convey to consumers that the product is environmentally superior to other products. If the manufacturer cannot substantiate this broad claim, the claim would be deceptive. The claims would not be deceptive if they were accompanied by clear and prominent qualifying language limiting the environmental superiority representation to the particular product attribute or attributes for which they could be substantiated, provided that no other deceptive implications were created by the context.

Example 6: A product is advertised as "environmentally preferable." This claim is likely to convey to consumers that this product is environmentally superior to other products. If the manufacturer cannot substantiate this broad claim, the claim would be deceptive. The claim would not be deceptive if it were accompanied by clear and prominent qualifying language limiting the environmental superiority representation to the particular product attribute or attributes for which it could be substantiated, provided that no other deceptive implications were created by the context.

(b) Degradable/Biodegradable/Photodegradable: It is deceptive to misrepresent, directly or by implication, that a product or package is degradable, biodegradable or photodegradable. An unqualified claim that a product or package is degradable, biodegradable or photodegradable should be substantiated by competent and reliable scientific evidence that the entire product or package will completely break down and return to nature, *i.e.,*

decompose into elements found in nature within a reasonably short period of time after customary disposal.

Claims of degradability, biodegradability or photodegradability should be qualified to the extent necessary to avoid consumer deception about: (a) the product or package's ability to degrade in the environment where it is customarily disposed; and (b) the rate and extent of degradation.

Example 1: A trash bag is marketed as "degradable," with no qualification or other disclosure. The marketer relies on soil burial tests to show that the product will decompose in the presence of water and oxygen. The trash bags are customarily disposed of in incineration facilities or at sanitary landfills that are managed in a way that inhibits degradation by minimizing moisture and oxygen. Degradation will be irrelevant for those trash bags that are incinerated and, for those disposed of in landfills, the marketer does not possess adequate substantiation that the bags will degrade in a reasonably short period of time in a landfill. The claim is therefore deceptive.

Example 2: A commercial agricultural plastic mulch film is advertised as "Photodegradable" and qualified with the phrase, "Will break down into small pieces if left uncovered in sunlight." The claim is supported by competent and reliable scientific evidence that the product will break down in a reasonably short period of time after being exposed to sunlight and into sufficiently small pieces to become part of the soil. The qualified claim is not deceptive. Because the claim is qualified to indicate the limited extent of breakdown, the advertiser need not meet the elements for an unqualified photodegradable claim, *i.e.*, that the product will not only break down, but also will decompose into elements found in nature.

Example 3: A soap or shampoo product is advertised as "biodegradable," with no qualification or other disclosure. The manufacturer has competent and reliable scientific evidence demonstrating that the product, which is customarily disposed of in sewage systems, will break down and decompose into elements found in nature in a short period of time. The claim is not deceptive.

Example 4: A plastic six-pack ring carrier is marked with a small diamond. Many state laws require that plastic six-pack ring carriers degrade if littered, and several state laws also require that the carriers be marked with a small diamond symbol to indicate that they meet performance standards for degradability. The use of the diamond, by itself, does not constitute a claim of degradability.[3]

(c) Compostable: It is deceptive to misrepresent, directly or by implication, that a product or package is compostable. An unqualified claim that a product or package is compostable should be substantiated by competent and reliable scientific evidence that all the materials in the product or package will break down into, or otherwise become part of, usable compost (e.g., soil-conditioning material, mulch) in a safe and timely manner in an appropriate composting program or facility, or in a home compost pile or device.

Claims of compostability should be qualified to the extent necessary to avoid consumer deception. An unqualified claim may be deceptive: (1) if municipal composting facilities are not available to a substantial majority of consumers or communities where the package is sold; (2) if the claim misleads consumers about the environmental benefit provided when the product is disposed of in a landfill; or (3) if consumers misunderstand the claim to mean that the package can be safely composted in their home compost pile or device, when in fact it cannot.

Example 1: A manufacturer indicates that its unbleached coffee filter is compostable. The unqualified claim is not deceptive provided the manufacturer can substantiate that the filter can be converted safely to usable compost in a timely manner in a home compost pile or device, as well as in an appropriate composting program or facility.

Example 2: A lawn and leaf bag is labeled as "Compostable in

California Municipal Yard Waste Composting Facilities." The bag contains toxic ingredients that are released into the compost material as the bag breaks down. The claim is deceptive if the presence of these toxic ingredients prevents the compost from being usable.

Example 3: A manufacturer indicates that its paper plate is suitable for home composting. If the manufacturer possesses substantiation for claiming that the paper plate can be converted safely to usable compost in a home compost pile or device, this claim is not deceptive even if no municipal composting facilities exist.

Example 4: A manufacturer makes an unqualified claim that its package is compostable. Although municipal composting facilities exist where the product is sold, the package will not break down into usable compost in a home compost pile or device. To avoid deception, the manufacturer should disclose that the package is not suitable for home composting.

Example 5: A nationally marketed lawn and leaf bag is labeled "compostable." Also printed on the bag is a disclosure that the bag is not designed for use in home compost piles. The bags are in fact composted in municipal yard waste composting programs in many communities around the country, but such programs are not available to a substantial majority of consumers where the bag is sold. The claim is deceptive since reasonable consumers living in areas not served by municipal yard waste programs may understand the reference to mean that composting facilities accepting the bags are available in their area. To avoid deception, the claim should be qualified to indicate the limited availability of such programs, for example, by stating, "Appropriate facilities may not exist in your area." Other examples of adequate qualification of the claim include providing the approximate percentage of communities or the population for which such programs are available.

Example 6: A manufacturer sells a disposable diaper that bears the legend "This diaper can be composted where municipal solid waste composting facilities exist. There are currently [X number of] municipal solid waste composting facilities across the country."

The claim is not deceptive, assuming that composting facilities are available as claimed and the manufacturer can substantiate that the diaper can be converted safely to usable compost in municipal solid waste composting facilities.

Example 7: A manufacturer markets yard waste bags only to consumers residing in particular geographic areas served by county yard waste composting programs. The bags meet specifications for these programs and are labeled "Compostable Yard Waste Bag for County Composting Programs." The claim is not deceptive. Because the bags are compostable where they are sold, no qualification is required to indicate the limited availability of composting facilities.

(d) Recyclable: It is deceptive to misrepresent, directly or by implication, that a product or package is recyclable. A product or package should not be marketed as recyclable unless it can be collected, separated or otherwise recovered from the solid waste stream for use in the form of raw materials in the manufacture or assembly of a new package or product. Unqualified claims of recyclability for a product or package may be made if the entire product or package, excluding minor incidental components, is recyclable. For products or packages that are make of both recyclable and non-recyclable components, the recyclable claim should be adequately qualified to avoid consumer deception about which portions or components of the product or package are recyclable.

Claims of recyclability should be qualified to the extent necessary to avoid consumer deception about any limited availability of recycling programs and collections sites. If an incidental component significantly limits the ability to recycle the product, the claim would be deceptive. A product or package that is made from recyclable material, but, because of its shape, size or some other attribute, is not accepted in recycling programs for such material, should not be marketed as recyclable.

Example 1: A packaged product is labeled with an unqualified claim, "recyclable." It is unclear from the type of product and other context whether the claim refers to the product or its package. The unqualified claim is likely to convey to reasonable consumers that all of both the product and its packaging that remain after normal use of the product, except for minor, incidental components, can be recycled. Unless each such message can be substantiated, the claim should be qualified to indicate what portions are recyclable.

Example 2: A plastic package is labeled on the bottom with the Society of the Plastics Industry (SPI) code, consisting of a design of arrows in a triangular shape containing a number and abbreviation identifying the component plastic resin. Without more, the use of the SPI symbol (or similar industry codes) on the bottom of the package, or in a similarly inconspicuous location, does not constitute a claim of recyclability.

Example 3: A container can be burned in incinerator facilities to produce heat and power. It cannot, however, be recycled into new products or packaging. Any claim that the container is recyclable would be deceptive.

Example 4: A nationally marketed bottle bears the unqualified statement that it is "recyclable." Collection sites for recycling the material in question are not available to a substantial majority of consumers or communities, although collection sites are established in a significant percentage of communities or available to a significant percentage of the population. The unqualified claim is deceptive since, unless evidence shows otherwise, reasonable consumers living in communities not served by programs may conclude that recycling programs for the material are available in their area. To avoid deception, the claim should be qualified to indicate the limited availability of programs, for example, by stating "Check to see if recycling facilities exist in your area." Other examples of adequate qualifications of the claim include providing the approximate percentage of communities or the population to whom programs are available.

Example 5: A soda bottle is marketed nationally and labeled "Recyclable where facilities exist." Recycling programs for material of this type and size are available in a significant percentage of communities or to a significant percentage of the population, but are not available to a substantial majority of consumers. The claim is deceptive since, unless evidence shows otherwise, reasonable consumers living in communities not served by programs may understand this phrase to mean that programs are available in their area. To avoid deception, the claim should be further qualified to indicate the limited availability of programs, for example, by using any of the approaches set forth in Example 4 above.

Example 6: A plastic detergent bottle is marketed as follows: "Recyclable in the few communities with facilities for colored HDPE bottles." Collection sites for recycling the container have been established in a half-dozen major metropolitan areas. This disclosure illustrates one approach to qualifying a claim adequately to prevent deception about the limited availability of recycling programs where collection facilities are not established in a significant percentage of communities or available to a significant percentage of the population. Other examples of adequate qualification of the claim include providing the number of communities with programs, or the percentage of communities or the population to which programs are available.

Example 7: A label claims that the package "includes some recyclable material." The package is composed of four layers of different materials, bonded together. One of the layers is made from the recyclable material, but the others are not. While programs for recycling this type of material are available to a substantial majority of consumers, only a few of those programs have the capability to separate out the recyclable layer. Even though it is technologically possible to separate the layers, the claim is not adequately qualified to avoid consumer deception. An appropriately qualified claim would be "includes material recyclable in the few communities that collect multi-layer products." Other examples of adequate qualification of the claim include providing the number of communities with programs, or the percentage of communities or the population to which programs are available.

Example 8: A product is marketed as having a "recyclable" container. The product is distributed and advertised only in Missouri. Collection sites for recycling the container are available to a substantial majority of Missouri residents, but are not yet available nationally. Because programs are generally available where the product is marketed, the unqualified claim does not deceive consumers about the limited availability of recycling programs.

(e) Recycled Content: A recycled content claim may be made only for materials that have been recovered or otherwise diverted from the solid waste stream, either during the manufacturing process (pre-consumer), or after consumer use (post-consumer). To the extent the source of recycled content includes pre-consumer material, the manufacturer or advertiser must have substantiation for concluding that the pre-consumer material would otherwise have entered the solid waste stream. In asserting a recycled content claim, distinctions may be made between pre-consumer and post-consumer materials. Where such distinctions are asserted, any express or implied claim about the specific pre-consumer or post-consumer content of a product or package must be substantiated.

It is deceptive to misrepresent, directly or by implication, that a product or package is made of recycled material. Unqualified claims of recycled content may be made only if the entire product or package, excluding minor, incidental components, is made from recycled material. For products or packages that are only partially made of recycled material, a recycled claim should be adequately qualified to avoid consumer deception about the amount, by weight, of recycled content in the finished product or package.

Example 1: A manufacturer routinely collects spilled raw material and scraps left over from the original manufacturing process.

After a minimal amount of reprocessing, the manufacturer combines the spills and scraps with virgin material for use in further production of the same product. A claim that the product contains recycled material is deceptive since the spills and scraps to which the claim refers are normally reused by industry within the original manufacturing process, and would not normally have entered the waste stream.

Example 2: A manufacturer purchases material from a firm that collects discarded material from other manufacturers and resells it. All of the material was diverted from the solid waste stream and is not normally reused by industry within the original manufacturing process. The manufacturer includes the weight of this material in its calculations of the recycled content of its products. A claim of recycled content based on this calculation is not deceptive because, absent the purchase and reuse of this material, it would have entered the waste stream.

Example 3: A greeting card is composed 30% by fiber weight of paper collected from consumers after use of a paper product, and 20% by fiber weight of paper that was generated after completion of the paper-making process, diverted from the solid waste stream, and otherwise would not normally have been reused in the original manufacturing process. The marketer of the card may claim either that the product "contains 50% recycled fiber," or may identify the specific pre-consumer and/or post-consumer content by stating, for example, that the product "contains 50% total recycled fiber, including 30% post-consumer."

Example 4: A paperboard package with 20% recycled fiber by weight is labeled as containing "20% recycled fiber." Some of the recycled content was composed of material collected from consumers after use of the original product. The rest was composed of overrun newspaper stock never sold to customers. The claim is not deceptive.

Example 5: A product in a multi-component package, such as a paperboard box in a shrink-wrapped plastic cover, indicates that it has recycled packaging. The paperboard box is made entirely of recycled material, but the plastic cover is not. The claim is deceptive since, without qualification, it suggests that both components are recycled. A claim limited to the paperboard box would not be deceptive.

Example 6: A package is made from layers of foil, plastic, and paper laminated together, although the layers are indistinguishable to consumers. The label claims that "one of the three layers of this package is made of recycled plastic." The plastic layer is made entirely of recycled plastic. The claim is not deceptive provided the recycled plastic layer constitutes a significant component of the entire package.

Example 7: A paper product is labeled as containing "100% recycled fiber." The claim is not deceptive if the advertiser can substantiate the conclusion that 100% by weight of the fiber in the finished product is recycled.

Example 8: A frozen dinner is marketed in a package composed of a cardboard box over a plastic tray. The package bears the legend "package made from 30% recycled material." Each packaging component amounts to one-half the weight of the total package. The box is 20% recycled content by weight, while the plastic tray is 40% recycled content by weight. The claim is not deceptive, since the average amount of recycled material is 30%.

Example 9: A paper greeting card is labeled as containing 50% recycled fiber. The seller purchases paper stock from several sources and the amount of recycled fiber in the stock provided by each source varies. Because the 50% figure is based on the annual weighted average of recycled material purchased from the sources after accounting for fiber loss during the production process, the claim is permissible.

Example 10: A packaged food product is labeled with a three chasing arrows symbol without any further explanatory text as to its meaning. By itself, the symbol is likely to convey that the packaging is both "recyclable" and is made entirely from recycled material. Unless both messages can be substantiated, the claim should be qualified as to whether it refers to the package's recyclability and/or its recycled content. If a "recyclable claim" is being made, the label may need to disclose the limited availability of recycling programs for the package. If a recycled content claim is being made and the packaging is not made entirely from recycled material, the label should disclose the percentage of recycled content.

(f) Source Reduction: It is deceptive to misrepresent, directly or by implication, that a product or package has been reduced or is lower in weight, volume or toxicity. Source reduction claims should be qualified to the extent necessary to avoid consumer deception about the amount of the source reduction and about the basis for any comparison asserted.

Example 1: An ad claims that solid waste created by disposal of the advertiser's packaging is "now 10% less than our previous package." The claim is not deceptive if the advertiser has substantiation that shows that disposal of the current package contributes 10% less waste by weight or volume to the solid waste stream when compared with the immediately preceding version of the package.

Example 2: An advertiser notes that disposal of its product generates "10% less waste." The claim is ambiguous. Depending on contextual factors, it could be a comparison either to the immediately preceding product or to a competitor's product. The "10% less waste" reference is deceptive unless the seller clarifies which comparison is intended and substantiates that comparison, or substantiates both possible interpretations of the claim.

(g) Refillable: It is deceptive to misrepresent, directly or by implication, that a package is refillable. An unqualified refillable claim should not be asserted unless a system is provided for: (1) the collection and return of the package for refill; or (2) the later refill of the package by consumers with product subsequently sold in another package. A package should not be marketed with an

unqualified refillable claim, if it is up to the consumer to find new ways to refill the package.

Example 1: A container is labeled "refillable x times." The manufacturer has the capability to refill returned containers and can show that the container will withstand being refilled at least x times. The manufacturer, however, has established no collection program. The unqualified claim is deceptive because there is no means for collection and return of the container to the manufacturer for refill.

Example 2: A bottle of fabric softener states that it is in a "handy refillable container." The manufacturer also sells a large-sized container that indicates that the consumer is expected to use it to refill the smaller container. The manufacturer sells the large-sized container in the same market areas where it sells the small container. The claim is not deceptive because there is a means for consumers to refill the smaller container from larger containers of the same product.

(h) *Ozone Safe and Ozone Friendly*: It is deceptive to misrepresent, directly or by implication, that a product is safe for or "friendly" to the ozone layer or the atmosphere.

For example, a claim that a product does not harm the ozone layer is deceptive if the product contains an ozone-depleting substance.

Example 1: A product is labeled "ozone friendly." The claim is deceptive if the product contains any ozone-depleting substance, including those substances listed as Class I or Class II chemicals in Title VI of the Clean Air Act Amendments of 1990, Pub. L. No. 101–549, and others subsequently designated by EPA as ozone-depleting substances. Chemicals that have been listed or designated as Class I are chlorofluorocarbons (CFCs), halons, carbon tetrachloride, 1,1,1-trichloroethane, methyl bromide and hydrobromofluorocarbons (HBFCs). Chemicals that have been listed as Class II are hydrochlorofluorocarbons (HCFCs).

Example 2: An aerosol air freshener is labeled "ozone friendly." Some of the product's ingredients are volatile organic compounds (VOCs) that may cause smog by contributing to ground-level ozone formation. The claim is likely to convey to consumers that the product is safe for the atmosphere as a whole, and is therefore deceptive.

Example 3: The seller of an aerosol product makes an unqualified claim that its product "Contains no CFCs." Although the product does not contain CFCs, it does contain HCFC-22, another ozone depleting ingredient. Because the claim "Contains no CFCs" may imply to reasonable consumers that the product does not harm the ozone layer, the claim is deceptive.

Example 4: A product is labeled "This product is 95% less damaging to the ozone layer than past formulations that contained CFCs." The manufacturer has substituted HCFCs for CFC-12, and can substantiate that this substitution will result in 95% less ozone depletion. The qualified comparative claim is not likely to be deceptive.

260.8 Environmental assessment

NATIONAL ENVIRONMENTAL POLICY ACT: In accordance with section 1.83 of the FTC's Procedures and Rules of Practice[4] and section 1501.3 of the Council on Environmental Quality's regulations for implementing the procedural provisions of National Environmental Policy Act, 42 U.S.C. 4321 *et seq.* (1969),[5] the Commission prepared an environmental assessment when the guides were issued in July 1992 for purposes of providing sufficient evidence and analysis to determine whether issuing the Guides for the Use of Environmental Marketing Claims required preparation of an environmental impact statement or a finding of no significant impact. After careful study, the Commission concluded that issuance of the Guides would not have a significant impact on the environment and that any such impact "would be so uncertain that environmental analysis would be based on speculation."[6] The Commission concluded that an environmental impact statement was therefore not required. The Commission based its conclusions on the findings in the environmental assessment that issuance of the guides would have no quantifiable environmental impact because the guides are voluntary in nature, do not preempt inconsistent state laws, are based on the FTC's deception policy, and, when used in conjunction with the Commission's policy of case-by-case enforcement, are intended to aid compliance with section 5(a) of the FTC Act as that Act applies to environmental marketing claims.

The Commission has concluded that the modifications proposed to the guides in this Notice will not have a significant effect on the environment, for the same reasons that the issuance of the original guides in 1992 were deemed not to have a significant effect on the environment. Therefore, the Commission concludes that an environmental impact statement is not required in conjunction with the issuance of these modifications to the Guides for the Use of Environmental Marketing Claims.

By direction of the Commission.

Donald S. Clark
Secretary

Notes

1. *Cliffdale Associates, Inc.*, 103 F.T.C. 100, at 176, 176 n.7, n.8, Appendix, *reprinting* letter dated Oct. 14, 1983, from the Commission to The Honorable John D. Dingell, Chairman, Committee on Energy and Commerce, U.S. House of Representatives (1984) ("Deception Statement").
2. These guides do not currently address claims based on a "life cycle" theory of environmental benefit. The Commission lacks sufficient information on which to base guidance on such claims.

3. The guides' treatment of unqualified degradable claims is intended to help prevent consumer deception and is not intended to establish performance standards for laws intended to ensure the degradability of products when littered.

4. 16 C.F.R. 1.83 (revised as of January 1, 1991).

5. 40 C.F.R. 1501.3 (1991).

6. 16 C.F.R. 1.83(a).

For Further Reading

CONSUMER RESOURCES

Alternative Energy Sourcebook, John Schaeffer, ed., Real Goods Trading Corporation, 966 Mazzoni Street, Ukiah, CA 95482-3471. 9th edition, 1996.

Consumer Co-op America Quarterly, 1612 K Street NW, Suite 600, Washington, DC 20006.

Co-op America's National Green Pages, Rosemary Brown, ed., Co-op America, 1612 K Street NW, Washington, DC 20006.

E. The Environmental Magazine, Doug Moss, ed., Earth Action Network, P.O. Box 5098, Westport, CT 06851.

Mother Jones Magazine, 731 Market Street, Suite 600, San Francisco, CA 94103.

Shopping for a Better World: A Quick and Easy Guide to Socially Responsible Supermarket Shopping, Benjamin Hollister et al., Council on Economic Priorities, New York, NY, 1994.

Sierra, Jonathan F. King, ed., Sierra Club, 730 Polk Street, San Francisco, CA 94109.

Simple Living: The Journal of Voluntary Simplicity, Janet Lahrs, ed., Simple Living Press, 2319 N. 45th Street, Box 149, Seattle, WA 98103.

Voluntary Simplicity: Toward a New Way of Life That Is Outwardly Simple, Inwardly Rich, Duane Elgin, William Morrow & Co., New York, NY, 1981.

Your Money or Your Life: Transforming Your Relationship with Money and Achieving Financial Independence, Vicki Robin and Joe Dominiquez, Penguin Books, 1992.

BUSINESS RESOURCES

Biologic: Environmental Protection by Design, David Wann, author. Johnson Publishing Company. 1880 S. 57 Court, Boulder, CO 80301. 1990.

Build It with Bale, 2nd edition, Matts Myhrman and Stephen MacDonald. Out on Bale, Tucson, AZ.

Business and the Environment, monthly newsletter, Kathleen M. Victory, ed., Cutter Information Corp., Arlington, MA.

Business Ethics: The Magazine of Socially Responsible Business, Marjorie Kelly, ed., Mavis Publications, Inc., 52 S. 10th St. #110, Minneapolis, MN 55403.

The Carbohydrate Economy: Making Chemicals and Industrial Materials from Plant Matter, David Morris and Irshad Ahmed, The Institute of Local Self-Reliance, 1992, 2425 18th Street NW, Washington, DC 20009-2096.

The Consumer's Guide to Planet Earth, 8th edition, Schultz Communications, 9412 Admiral Nimitz NE, Dept. CG8, Albuquerque, NM 87111.

Deep Design: Pathways to a Livable Future, David Wann, Island Press, Washington, DC 20009, 1996.

Designing Work for Sustainability, International Institute for Sustainable Development, 161 Portage Avenue East, 6th Floor, Winnipeg, Manitoba, Canada, R3B 0Y4, 1994.

Determinants of Effectiveness for Environmental Certification and Labeling Programs, U.S. EPA Office of Pollution Prevention and Toxics, April 1994, EPA 742-R-94-001.

Earth Enterprise Tool Kit, Institute for Sustainable Development, Winnipeg, Manitoba, Canada.

The Ecology of Commerce: A Declaration of Sustainability, Paul Hawken, Harper Business Books, New York, 1993.

The Environmental Entrepreneur: Where to Find the Profit in Saving the Earth, John Thompson, Longstreet Press, Atlanta, Georgia, 1992.

Environmental Marketing: Strategies, Practice, Theory, and Research, Michael J. Polonsky and Alma T. Mintu-Wimsatt, eds., The Haworth Press, Inc., New York, 1995.

Environmental Values in American Culture, Willett Kempton, James S. Boster, and Jennifer A. Hartley, The MIT Press, Cambridge, MA, 1995.

Germany, Garbage, and the Green Dot: Challenging the Throwaway Society, Bette K. Fishbein, Inform, Inc., New York, NY 10016-8806, 1994.

Green at Work: Finding a Business Career That Works for the Environment, Susan Cohn, Island Press, Washington, DC 20009, 1995.

The Green Business Letter, Joel Makower, ed., Tilden Press, Inc., 1519 Connecticut Avenue NW, Washington, DC 20036.

Green Marketing and Management—a Global Perspective, John F. Wasik, Blackwell Publishers, 238 Main Street, Cambridge, MA 02142, 1996.

Green Pricing Newsletter, Ed Holt, ed., The Regulatory Assistance Project, 177 Water Street, Gardiner, ME 04345-2149.

Greener Marketing & Advertising: Charting a Responsible Course, Robert Rehak, ed., Rodale Press, 1993, Ogilvy and Mather, Houston, TX.

In Business: The Magazine for Environmental Entrepreneuring, Jerome Goldstein, ed., JG Press, Inc., 419 State Avenue, Emmaus, PA 18049.

The Last Straw Journal, Tom Hahn, ed., Out on Bale, Tucson, AZ.

Lean and Clean Management: How to Boost Profits and Productivity by Reducing Pollution, Joseph L. Romm, Kodansha America, Inc., New York, NY 10011, 1994.

Life Cycle Design Guidance Manual: Environmental Requirements and the Product System, Gregory Keoleian and Dan Menerey, National Pollution Prevention Center, U.S. Environmental Protection Agency, January 1993, EPA/600/R-92/226.

Product Development and the Environment, Paul Burall, Gower Publishing, Brookfield, VT 05036, 1996.

Recycled Products Business Letter, Alan S. Orloff, ed., Environmental Newsletters, Inc., 11906 Paradise Lane, Herndon, VA 22071-1519.

The Recyclers' Directory, Resource Recycling, P.O. Box 10540, Portland, OR 97296.

Road to 2015, John L. Petersen, ed., Waite Group Press, 200 Tamal Plaza, Corte Madera, CA 94925.

The Soul of a Business: Managing for Profit and the Common Good, Tom Chappell, Bantam, Doubleday and Dell Publishers, New York, NY, 1992.

State Recycling Laws Update, Michelle Raymond, ed., Raymond Communications, Riverdale, MD.

Status Report on the Use of Environmental Labels Worldwide, U.S. EPA Office of Pollution Prevention and Toxics, September 1993, EPA 742-R-9-93-001.

Tomorrow: Global Environmental Business, Claes Sjoberg, editor-in-chief, Tomorrow Media, 2000 Broadway, Suite 273, Redwood City, CA 94063.

General Resources

Conservation Directory of Environmental Organizations, National Wildlife Federation, 8925 Leesburg Pike, Vienna, VA 22184, 1997.

State of the World 1996, Lester Brown et al., W. W. Norton & Company, New York, NY, 1996.

World Watch magazine, Worldwatch Institute, 1776 Massachusetts Avenue NW, Washington, DC 20036.

For Further Information

AFM Enterprises, Inc.
350 West Ash Street
Suite 700
San Diego, CA 92101
(619) 239-0321

**Alternative Agricultural
Research Commercialization
Corp.**
1400 Independence Avenue SW
Room 0156, South Building
Washington, DC 20250-0401
(202) 690-1633

**American Marketing
Association**
250 South Wacker Drive
Chicago, IL 60606
(800) AMA-1150

American Rivers
801 Pennsylvania Avenue
Washington, DC 20003
(202) 547-6900

Amicus Journal
40 West 20th Street
New York, NY 10011
(212) 727-2700

Amway
7575 East Fulton Road
Ada, MI 49355
(616) 676-6000

Annie's Homegrown
Box 128
Hampton, CT 06247
(203) 455-0276

Apple Computer
10455 Bundley Drive
Cupertino, CA 95014
(408) 996-1010

ARCO
515 South Flower Street
Los Angeles, CA 90071
(213) 486-3511

ASKO USA, Inc.
1161 Executive West
Richardson, TX 75081
(972) 644-8595

AT&T
131 Morristown Road
Basking, NJ 07920
(908) 221-2000

Audubon **Magazine**
700 Broadway
New York, NY 10003
(212) 979-3000

Aveda
4000 Pheasant Ridge Drive
Blaine, MN 55449
(800) AVEDA-24

Banana Republic, Inc.
2 Harrison Street
San Francisco, CA 94105
(415) 777-0250

Battelle
505 King Avenue
Columbus, OH 43201
(614) 424-4463

Ben & Jerry's Homemade
Route 100
Waterbury, VT 05676
(802) 244-5641

Bethlehem Steel
1170 8th Avenue
Bethlehem, PA 18016
(610) 694-2424

The Body Shop
Watersmead
West Sussex, England
BN 17 6LS

Boston Globe
135 William T. Morris
  Boulevard
Dorchester, MA 02125
(617) 929-2000

Bristol-Myers
345 Park Avenue
New York, NY 10154
(212) 546-4000

Canon
1 Canon Place
Lake Success, NY 11042
(516) 328-5000

Captain Planet
Turner Broadcasting
1 CNN Center
Atlanta, GA 30303
(404) 827-3300

Cargill
15407 McGinty Road West
Wayzata, MN 55391
(612) 742-6773

Carrier
A&R Building
Carrier Parkway
P.O. Box 4808
Syracuse, NY 13221
(315) 432-6000

Chemical Manufacturers
Association
1300 Wilson Boulevard
Arlington, VA 22209
(703) 741-5000

Chemical Specialties
Manufacturers Association
1913 Eye Street NW
Washington, DC 20006
(202) 872-8110

Chevron
P.O. Box 7753
San Francisco, CA 94120
(415) 894-7700

Church & Dwight
469 North Harrison Street
Princeton, NJ 08543
(609) 683-5900

Coalition for
Environmentally Responsible
Economies (CERES)
711 Atlantic Avenue, 5th Floor
Boston, MA 02111
(617) 451-0927
ceres@igc.apc.org

Coca-Cola
One Coca-Cola Plaza
P.O. Drawer 1734
Atlanta, GA 30301
(404) 676-2121

Colgate-Palmolive
300 Park Avenue
New York, NY 10022
(212) 310-2000

Collins Pine
1618 Southwest First Avenue
Suite 300
Portland, OR 97201
(800) 324-1219

Compaq Computer Corp.
P.O. Box 692000
Houston, TX 77269
(281) 370-0670

Competitive Media
11 West 42nd Street
New York, NY 10036
(212) 789-1400

The Conference Board
Townley Global Management
   Center for Environment,
   Health, and Safety
845 3rd Avenue
New York, NY 10010
(212) 759-0900

Conservation Alliance
6750 South 228th Street
Kent, WA 98023
(206) 395-5956

Corporate Conservation Council
8925 Leesburg Pike
Vienna, VA 22184-0001
(703) 790-4401
E-mail: cccaa@nwf.org
www.nwf.org/nwf/about/ccc.html

Council on Economic Priorities
30 Irving Place
New York, NY 10003
(212) 420-1133

Cpc International
P.O. Box 8000
Englewood, NJ 07632
(201) 894-4000

Crane and Company
30 South Street
Dalton, MA 01226
(413) 684-2600

Danka Worldwide Industries
3636 131st Avenue North
St. Petersburg, FL 33716
(813) 573-2911

Ddb Needham
437 Madison Avenue
New York, NY 10022
(212) 415-2000

Design Tex Inc.
200 Varick Street
New York, NY 10014
(800) 221-1540

Discovery Channel
7700 Wisconsin
Bethesda, MD 20785
(301) 986-1999

Dow Chemical Co.
2030 Willard H. Dow Center
Midland, MI 48674
(517) 636-1000

Duke University
Raleigh-Durham, NC 27708
(919) 684-8111

DuPont
1007 Market Street
Wilmington, DE 19898
(302) 774-4710

Earth's Best
4840 Pearl East Circle
Suite 201
Boulder, CO 80301
(303) 449-3780

Eastman Kodak
343 State Street
Rochester, NY 14650
(716) 724-4000

Eco Expo Online
14260 Ventura Boulevard
Suite 201
Sherman Oaks, CA 91423
(818) 906-2700
http://www.ecoexpo.com

Ecobalance
15204 Omega Drive
Suite 220
Rockville, MD 20850
(301) 548-1750

EcoMall
P.O. Box 20553
Cherokee Station
New York, NY 10021-0070
(212) 289-1234
http://www.ecomall.com

Ecomat
147 Palmer Avenue
Mamaroneck, NY 10543
(914) 777-3600

Edison International
2244 Walnut Grove Avenue
Rosemead, CA 91776
(626) 302-1212

Electric Power Research
Institute
2000 L Street NW
Washington, DC 20036
(202) 872-9222

Electrolux
2300 Wendy Ridge Parkway
Atlanta, GA 30339
(800) 243-9078

EnviroLink
4618 Henry Street
Pittsburgh, PA 15213
(412) 683-6400
http://www.envirolink.org

Environmental Defense Fund
257 Park Avenue South
New York, NY 10010
(212) 505-2100
www.edf.org

Esprit
900 Minnesota Street
San Francisco, CA 94107
(415) 648-6900

European Commission
Directorate-General for the
  Environment
200 rue de la Loi
1049 Brussels, Belgium
+32 2 295 6133

Exxon Corp.
5959 Las Colinas Boulevard
Erving, TX 75039
(972) 444-1000

Federal Trade Commission
6th Street & Pennsylvania
  Avenue NW
Washington, DC 20580
(202) 326-2000
http://www.ftc.gov

Fetzer Vineyards
P.O. Box 661
Hopland, CA 95449
(707) 485-7634

First Brands
39 Old Ridgebury
Danbury, CT 06817
(203) 731-2300

Forest Products Laboratory
1 Gifford Pinchot Drive
Madison, WI 53705-2398
(608) 231-9248
www.fpl.fs.fed.us/.

Franklin Associates
4121 West 83rd Street
Suite 108
Prairie Village, KS 66208
(913) 649-2225

Frigidaire Co.
6000 Perimeter Drive
Dublin, OH 43017-3215
(614) 792-2153

The Gallup Organization
100 Palmer Square
Suite 200
Princeton, NJ 08542
(609) 929-9600

The Gap, Inc.
900 Cherry Avenue
San Bruno, CA 94066
(800) 333-7899

Giessen Wolf
60 River Road
Weston, MA 02193
(617) 736-1822

General Electric
Nela Park
Cleveland, OH 44112
(216) 266-2000

General Motors
3044 West Grand Boulevard
Detroit, MI 48202
(313) 556-5000

Global Environmental Management Initiative
2000 L Street NW
Suite 710
Washington, DC 20036
(202) 296-7449
www.gemi.org

Goodkind Pen Co.
15 Holly Street
112 Pine Point Park
Scarborough, ME 04074
(207) 883-1259

Green Disk
8124 304 Avenue Southeast
Preston, WA 98050
(206) 222-7734

Green Logic Design and Consulting
P.O. Box 2249
New York, NY 10009
(212) 769-6387

Green Market
2301 California Street
Suite 603
San Francisco, CA 94111
(415) 544-0111

Green Mountain Energy Partners
P.O. Box 2206
South Burlington, VT 05407
(802) 846-6100

Green Seal
1400 16th Street NW
Suite 300
Washington, DC 20036
(202) 588-8400

Green Star
415 E Street
Suite 201
Anchorage, AK 99501
(907) 278-7827

Greenpeace
P.O. Box 77048
San Francisco, CA 94107
(800) 327-3223

Gridcore Systems International
1400 Canal Avenue
Long Beach, CA 90813
(310) 901-1492

GSD&M Advertising
1250 Capital of Texas Highway
Austin, TX 78746
(512) 327-8810

Habitat for Humanity
1773 East 4th Street
Long Beach, CA 90802
(562) 495-1954

The Harwood Group
4915 St. Elmo Avenue
Suite 402
Bethesda, MD 20814
(301) 656-3669

Heinz
1062 Progress Street
Pittsburg, PA 15212
(412) 456-5700

Henkel Corp.
300 Brookside Avenue
Ambler, PA 19002
(215) 628-1000

**Herman Miller Co. Home
Furnishing**
P.O. Box 302
855 East Main Street
Zeeland, MI 49464
(616) 654-3000

Hewlett-Packard Company
1501 Page Mill Road
Palo Alto, CA 94304-1213
(415) 857-1501

Home Depot
2727 Paces Ferry
Atlanta, GA 30339
(770) 433-8211

IBM
Route 100
Somers, NY 10589
(800) 426-4968

IEG, Inc.
640 North LaSalle
Suite 600
Chicago, IL 60610-3777
(312) 944-1727

IKEA North America
496 West Germantown Pike
Plymouth Meeting, PA 19462
(610) 834-0180

INC. **Magazine**
38 Commercial Wharf
Boston, MA 02110
(617) 248-8000

Institute of Ecolonomics
23835 Highway 550
Ridgeway, CO 81432
(970) 626-3861

Interface
2859 Paces Ferry
Suite 200
Atlanta, GA 30339
(770) 437-6800

**International Organization
for Standardization**
1 rue de Varembe
Case Postale 56
Switzerland
+41 22 749-0111

International Paper
2 Manhattanville
Purchase, NY 10577
(914) 397-1500

J. Ottman Consulting, Inc.
1133 Broadway
Suite 1211
New York, NY 10010
(212) 255-3800
ottman@greenmarketing.com
www.greenmarketing.com

John Deere, Inc.
400 North Vine
Horicon Works
Horicon, WI 53032
(920) 485-4411

Johnson & Johnson
Grandview Road
Skillman, NJ 08933
(908) 874-1000

K mart
3100 West Big Beaver
Troy, MI 48084
(313) 643-1000

The Knoll Group N.Y.C.
105 Wooster Street
New York, NY 10012
(212) 343-4000

Lever Brothers
390 Park Avenue
New York, NY 10022
(212) 688-6000

Levi's
1155 Battery Street
San Francisco, CA 94111
(415) 501-6000

Lexus
19001 South Western
Mail Drop L203
Torrance, CA 90509
(800) 255-3987

Matsushita Electric
One Panasonic Way
Secaucus, NJ 07094
(201) 348-7000

Mattel
333 Continental Boulevard
MS:M1-0605
El Segundo, CA 90245
(213) 524-2000

Maytag Corp.
403 West 4th Street, North
Newton, IA 50208
(515) 792-8000

Mazda
7755 Irvine Center Drive
Irvine, CA 92718
(714) 727-1990

McDonald's
1 Kroc Drive
Oakbrook, IL 60523
(630) 623-3000

Melitta
1401 Berlin Road
Cherry Hill, NJ 08003
(609) 428-7202

Merck Family Fund
6930 Carroll Avenue
Suite 500
Takoma Park, MD 20912
(301) 270-2970
Merck@ipg.apc.org

Millstone Coffee
729 100th Street
Everett, WA 98208
(206) 347-3995

Mobil
325 Gallows Road
Fairfax, VA 22037
(703) 848-2500

Montgomery Ward
535 West Chicago Avenue
Chicago, IL 60671
(312) 467-2000

Mother Jones **Magazine**
731 Market Street
Suite 600
San Francisco, CA 94103
(415) 357-0509

National Audubon Society
700 Broadway
New York, NY 10003
(212) 979-3000

**National Environmental and
Education Training
Foundation**
915 15th Street NW
Suite 200
Washington, DC 20005
(202) 628-8200

Natural Cotton Colours, Inc.
P.O. Box 66
Wickenburg, AZ 85358
(805) 758-3928

Natural Fibers Corp.
Airport Road
P.O. Box 830
Ogallala, NE 69153
(308) 284-8403

**Natural Resources Defense
Council**
40 West 20th Street
New York, NY 10010
(212) 727-2700

The Natural Step
4000 Bridgeway
Suite 102
Sausalito, CA 94965
(415) 332-9394

The Nature Conservancy
International Headquarters
1815 North Lynn Street
Arlington, VA 22209
(703) 841-5300

New York Times
229 West 43rd Street
New York, NY 10036
(212) 556-1234

Nissan
18600 South Figueroa
Carson, CA 90248
(310) 532-3111

Northface
1238 5th Street
Berkeley, CA 94710
(510) 526-3530

Out on Bale by Mail
1037 East Linden Street
Tucson, AZ 85719
(520) 624-1673

Outside **Magazine**
400 Market Street
Santa Fe, NM 87501
(800) 688-7433

Panasonic
2 Panasonic Way
Secaucus, NJ 07904
(201) 348-7000

Patagonia
259 West Santa Clara Street
Ventura, CA 93001
(805) 643-8616

**Peter D. Hart Research
Associates, Inc.**
1724 Connecticut Avenue NW
Washington, DC 20009
(202) 234-5570

Philip Morris
120 Park Avenue
New York, NY 10017
(212) 880-5000

Philips Lighting
200 Franklin Square
Franklin Lakes, NJ 08875
(908) 563-3000

Pitney-Bowes
27 Waterview Drive
Shelton, CT 06483
(203) 922-4000

**Planned Parenthood
Federation of America**
810 7th Avenue
New York, NY 10019
(212) 541-7800

Polaroid
549 Technology Street
Cambridge, MA 02139
(617) 386-2000

Procter & Gamble
One P & G Plaza
Cincinnati, OH 45201
(513) 983-1100

Prudential
751 Broad Street
16th Floor
Newark, NJ 07101
(201) 802-6000

Rayovac
P.O. Box 4960
Madison, WI 53711
(608) 275-3340

Real Goods Trading Co.
966 Mazzoni Street
Ukiah, CA 95482
(800) 762-7325

Reckitt & Colman
1655 Valley Road
P.O. Box 943
Wayne, NJ 07474
(201) 633-6700

Reebok International Ltd.
150 Royall Street
Canton, MA 02021
(617) 821-2800

Ricoh
Five Dedrick Place
West Caldwell, NJ 07006
(201) 882-2075

Rocky Mountain Institute
1739 Snowmass
Snowmass, CO 81654
(970) 927-3851

Roper Starch Worldwide
205 East 42nd Street
New York, NY 10017
(212) 599-0700

Rubbermaid
1147 Akron Road
Wooster, OH 44691
(216) 264-6464

S. C. Johnson
1525 Howe Street
Racine, WI 55403
(414) 631-2000

Safe Brands
55 Sierra Madre Boulevard
Sierra Madre, CA 91024
(818) 355-1050

Safety Kleen
777 Big Timber Road
Elgin, IL 60123
(847) 697-8460

Sanyo Energy Corporation
2001 Sanyo Avenue
San Diego, CA 92173
(619) 661-6620

Schroeder Milk Company
2080 Rice Street
St. Paul, MN 55113
(612) 487-1471

Scientific Certification Systems
The Ordway Building
One Kaiser Plaza
Suite 901
Oakland, CA 94612
(510) 832-1415

Sears
Sears Tower
Chicago, IL 60684
(312) 875-2500

Seventh Generation
1 Mill Street
P.O. Box A26
Burlington, VT 05401-1530 ·
(800) 456-1177

Shadow Lake, Inc.
188 Shadow Lake Road
Ridgefield, CT 06877-1032
(203) 778-0881

Sierra Club
730 Polk Street
San Francisco, CA 94109
(415) 977-5500

Solar Energy Industries Association
122 C Street NW
4th Floor
Washington, DC 20001
(202) 383-2600

Starkist
Division of Heinz
180 East Ocean Boulevard
Long Beach, CA 90802
(213) 590-7900

Stonyfield Farm
10 Burton Drive
Londonderry, NH 63053
(603) 437-4040

Sun Company
1801 Market Street
Philadelphia, PA 19103
(215) 977-3000

Target Stores
33 South Sixth Street
P.O. Box 1392
Minneapolis, MN 55440
(612) 304-6073

Teledyne
1730 East Prospect Street
Fort Collins, CO 80525
(303) 484-1352

Tellus Institute
89 Broad Street
14th Floor
Boston, MA 02110
(617) 266-5400

Texaco Corp.
P.O. Box 509
Beacon, NY 12508
(914) 235-4000

3M
3M Center
St. Paul, MN 55144
(612) 733-1110

Timberland
200 Domain Drive
Stratham, NH 03885
(800) 445-5545

Time Warner
75 Rockefeller Plaza
New York, NY 10019
(212) 484-8000

Tom's of Maine
Railroad Avenue
P.O. Box 710
Kennebunk, ME 04043
(207) 985-2944

Traverse City Light and Power
400 Boardman Avenue
Traverse City, MI 49685-0592
(616) 922-4470

Turner Broadcasting, Inc.
One CNN Center
Atlanta, GA 30303
(404) 827-1700

United Nations Environmental Programme
Working Group on Sustainable
  Product Development
International Center
University of Amsterdam
J. H. van Hoff Institute
Building B, 3rd Floor
Nieuve Achtergracht 166
1018 WV Amsterdam
The Netherlands
+31 20 525-6268

United States Department of Energy
1000 Independence Avenue SE
Washington, DC 20003
(202) 586-5000

United States Environmental Protection Agency
Atmospheric Pollution
  Prevention Division and
  ENERGY STAR Programs
401 M Street SW
Washington, DC 20460
(202) 382-2090

Utne Reader
1624 Harmon Place
Minneapolis, MN 55403
(612) 338-5040

Valspar Corp.
1191 South Wheeling Road
Wheeling, IL 60090
(847) 541-9000

Vision Paper
P.O. Box 20399
Albuquerque, NM 87154-0399
(505) 294-0293

Volvo of America
7 Volvo Drive
Rockleigh, NJ 07647
(201) 768-7300

Wal-Mart
702 Southwest 8th Street
Bentonville, AR 72716
(501) 273-4000

Waste Management, Inc.
3003 Butterfield Road
Oak Brook, IL 60521
(708) 572-8800

Wellman, Inc.
Shrewsbury Executive Center
1040 Broad Street
Suite 302
Shrewsbury, NJ 07702
(908) 542-7300

Weyerhaeuser
Tacoma, WA 98477
(206) 924-2345

Whirlpool
Administrative Center 2000 M-63N
Benton Harbor, MI 49022
(616) 926-5000

Worldwatch Institute
1776 Massachusetts Avenue
Washington, DC 20036
(202) 452-1999

Yankelovich, Clancy, and Shulman
8 Wright Street
Westport, CT 06877
(203) 277-2700

York International
P.O. Box 1592
York, PA 17405
(717) 771-7890

Xerox
Xerox Square-15A
Rochester, NY 14644
(800) 334-6200

Index

1992428